1-2-3 for Windows™ Quick Reference

Que Quick Reference Series

Joyce J. Nielsen

Revised by Janice A. Snyder

1-2-3 Release 5 for Windows Quick Reference

Copyright © 1994 by Que® Corporation

All rights reserved. Printed in the United States of America. No part of this book may be used or reproduced in any form or by any means, or stored in a database or retrieval system, without prior written permission of the publisher except in the case of brief quotations embodied in critical articles and reviews. Making copies of any part of this book for any purpose other than your own personal use is a violation of United States copyright laws. For information, address Que Corporation, 201 W. 103rd St., Indianapolis, IN 46290.

Library of Congress Catalog No.: 94-67040

ISBN: 1-56529-889-6

This book is sold *as is*, without warranty of any kind, either express or implied, respecting the contents of this book, including but not limited to implied warranties for the book's quality, performance, merchantability, or fitness for any particular purpose. Neither Que Corporation nor its dealers or distributors shall be liable to the purchaser or any other person or entity with respect to any liability, loss, or damage caused or alleged to have been caused directly or indirectly by this book.

96 95   5 4 3 2

Interpretation of the printing code: the rightmost double-digit number is the year of the book's printing; the rightmost single-digit number, the number of the book's printing. For example, a printing code of 94-1 shows that the first printing of the book occurred in 1994.

Screen reproductions in this book were created using Collage Complete from Inner Media, Inc., Hollis, NH.

All terms mentioned in this book that are known to be trademarks or service marks have been appropriately capitalized. Que cannot attest to the accuracy of this information. Use of a term in this book should not be regarded as affecting the validity of any trademark or service mark.

Publisher
David P. Ewing

Associate Publisher
Michael Miller

Publishing Director
Don Roche, Jr.

Managing Editor
Michael Cunningham

Acquisitions Editor
Thomas F. Godfrey III

Product Director
Joyce J. Nielsen

Production Editor
Lori A. Lyons

Technical Editor
Warren W. Estep

Acquisitions Coordinator
Deborah Abshier

Book Designer
Amy Peppler-Adams

Production Team
Stephen Adams, Angela Bannan, Cameron Booker,
Jenny Chung, Karen Dodson, Michael Thomas,
Tina Trettin, Donna Winter, Lillian Yates

Indexer
Bront Davis

Composed in *Stone* and *MCPdigital* by Que Corporation

Table of Contents

Introduction   **1**
    What Is 1-2-3 for Windows? 1
    New Features in 1-2-3 Release 5 for Windows 1
    Using This Book 2
    System Requirements 3
    Understanding Windows Basics 3
    1-2-3 for Windows Basics 6
    The 1-2-3 for Windows Screen 7
    Conventions Used in This Book 11

Task Reference   **13**
    Adding 13
    Aligning Data 13
    Approach 16
    Auditing Formulas 16
    Backsolver 18
    Bolding 20
    Borders 20
    Centering 22
    Changing the Working Directory 24
    Changing the Worksheet Display 24
    Charts 24
    Clearing Cells and Ranges 38
    Clip Art 38
    Clipboard 39
    Closing Files 40
    Colors 41
    Column Widths 41
    Combining Values from Separate Files 44
    Copying Data 46
    Creating Files 53
    Cross Tabulation 55
    Data Entry 55
    Database Management 55

Decimal Places	69
Deleting Files	71
Deleting Cells and Ranges	72
Deleting Rows, Columns, and Worksheets	72
Dialog Editor	73
Drawing	77
Editing Data	84
Entering Data	85
Erasing Cells and Ranges	88
Exiting 1-2-3 for Windows	90
Filling Ranges	90
Finding and Replacing Data	94
Fonts and Attributes	96
Formatting	97
Formulas	98
Freezing Titles	100
Frequency Distributions	101
Functions	102
Graphics	106
Grid Lines	107
Grouping Worksheets	108
Headers and Footers	109
Help	111
Hiding Data	112
Importing Data	112
Inserting Rows, Columns, and Worksheets	114
Installing 1-2-3 for Windows	115
Left Align	116
Lines and Colors	117
Linking Applications	118
Macros	122
Mapping	131
Margins	137
Matrices	137
Menus	138
Moving Data	142
Named Styles	146
Naming Files	147
Naming Ranges	149

Topic	Page
Naming Worksheets	151
Navigating the Worksheet	153
Notes	163
Number Formatting	164
Opening Files	169
Outlines	172
Passwords	172
Previewing Data	172
Printing Data	173
Protecting Files and Data	182
Recalculating a Worksheet	188
Regression Analysis	190
Right Align	192
Rounding	192
Row Heights	194
Saving Files	196
Sending Mail	199
SmartIcons	205
SmartMasters	213
Solver	217
Sorting Ranges	219
Specifying Ranges	221
Spell Checking	223
Splitting the Worksheet Window	224
Starting 1-2-3 for Windows	224
Style Gallery	226
Styling Data	226
Subtotals	227
Summing	227
Templates	228
Text Blocks	228
Totals	231
Underlining	231
Undo	234
Version Manager	234
What-If Tables	239
Worksheet Views	243
Zooming the Display	246
Index	247

Introduction

Welcome to *1-2-3 Release 5 for Windows Quick Reference*. This book is designed as a handy guide and reference for both new and experienced users of Lotus 1-2-3 Release 5 for Windows software. This book assumes a familiarity with Microsoft Windows, but does not assume that you have ever used 1-2-3 for Windows.

What Is 1-2-3 for Windows?

1-2-3 Release 5 for Windows is a full-featured spreadsheet program designed to run in Microsoft Windows 3.1 or 3.11. 1-2-3 Release 5 for Windows uses the graphical power of Windows to give you full visual access to your data so that you can easily view and work with it.

1-2-3 Release 5 for Windows functions similarly to other versions of 1-2-3 and can be used for simple applications or for complex financial planning. The program organizes data and includes such typical database functions as sorting, extracting, and finding data, as well as the capability to access external databases. Using 1-2-3 for Windows, you can produce graphic representations of financial and scientific data and create macros that automate common worksheet tasks.

New Features in 1-2-3 Release 5 for Windows

Release 5 of 1-2-3 for Windows is an update to Release 4, incorporating enhancements to Release 4 and additional features. Release 5 includes the following new features:

- Further improvement of information sharing, allowing exchange of data between 1-2-3 for Windows and Lotus Notes Release 3.0 or later, and range routing using electronic mail.

- Improved data analysis with interface to Lotus Approach Release 3.0 or later.

- The capability to link worksheet data to a geographical map.

- Several new macro commands and 16 new and/or enhanced @functions.

- Automatic update of file links when a worksheet file is opened.

- SmartMasters worksheet templates for instant layout of several common business and financial applications.

- Improved Help, including bubble descriptions when the mouse pointer is placed over a SmartIcon.

- Doc Info to track information about files, including title, subject, creation and revision information, keywords, and comments.

Using This Book

1-2-3 Release 5 for Windows Quick Reference is organized alphabetically by task. When you are working in 1-2-3 for Windows and get stuck, or you simply want some guidance before you get started, look at the heads at the top of each page to locate the appropriate section. Alternatively, you can use the Table of Contents at the beginning of the book, or the Index at the back of the book to assist you in locating the information you need.

This reference covers in a quick and concise manner all the tasks performed most often in 1-2-3 for Windows. If you need more-detailed information, however, Que's *Using 1-2-3 Release 5 for Windows*, Special Edition, provides the best and most complete coverage available of 1-2-3 Release 5 for Windows.

System Requirements

Before you install 1-2-3 Release 5 for Windows, make sure that your computer meets the following hardware, storage, and memory requirements:

- A system with 80386 (or higher) architecture
- A VGA or higher graphics card
- Microsoft Windows Version 3.1 or 3.11, running with DOS Version 3.3 or higher
- A minimum of 4M of RAM; maps and integration with Approach require 6M of RAM
- 14M available hard disk storage for the 1-2-3 Release 5 for Windows program only; 18M of available hard disk storage to install the 1-2-3 Release 5 for Windows program, additional program features, Help and sample files, and DataLens drivers

The following items are optional but recommended:

- A printer (any printer supported by Windows 3.1 or 3.11)
- A mouse (highly recommended)

To install 1-2-3 for Windows, see "Installing 1-2-3 for Windows" in the Task Reference.

Understanding Windows Basics

The following basic information should help you understand how Microsoft Windows works with 1-2-3 for Windows.

To enlarge or reduce windows

When you *maximize* the 1-2-3 window, it fills the screen. When you maximize the Worksheet window and other windows within the 1-2-3 window, each window fills the work area of the 1-2-3 window. You can enlarge or reduce a window by clicking the Minimize or Maximize button in the upper right corner of the window. You can also choose Maximize or Minimize from the Worksheet Control menu box.

To move windows

You can move a window or its icon. Moving a window is easiest with the mouse: click the title bar and drag the window to its new location. If the window is minimized, you can click the window's icon and drag it to a new position. With the keyboard, choose the Move command from the appropriate Control menu, use the direction keys to relocate the window, and press Enter.

To close windows

You can double-click the 1-2-3 Control menu box to close the 1-2-3 window or double-click the Worksheet Control menu box to close a Worksheet window. Each window's Control menu has a Close command that also enables you to close the window.

Shortcut
Press Alt+F4 to quickly close the 1-2-3 window. Press Ctrl+F4 to close the current Worksheet window.

If you have made any changes to a window and haven't saved them before you select the Close command, a dialog box prompts you to save any files before closing the window.

To cascade windows

Choose the Window Cascade command to arrange open windows so that they appear on top of one another, with only their title bars and the left edges of the windows showing. The active window always appears on top. To move between cascaded windows, press Ctrl+F6. You can change the size and location of the cascaded windows as described in the preceding sections.

Shortcut
Click the Cascade Windows SmartIcon.

To tile windows

Choose the Window Tile command to size and arrange all open windows side by side, like floor tiles. The active window's title bar is highlighted. To move between tiled windows, press Ctrl+F6.

Shortcut
Click the Tile Windows SmartIcon.

To choose a window display mode

In addition to the display-mode options described in the preceding sections, 1-2-3 for Windows offers other choices for displaying Worksheet windows. The following guidelines may help you select the best display mode for your worksheets:

- Maximizing the window provides the largest visible work area.

- Tiling the windows enables you to view portions of several files at the same time.

- Cascading the windows provides a large visible work area for the current window and makes switching between files easy.

- To display two views of the same worksheet, use the View Split Horizontal or View Split Vertical commands.

- To view three worksheets in a multiple-worksheet file, use View Split Perspective.

The View Set View Preferences command enables you to further control the display of a Worksheet window. Use this command to specify whether grid lines are displayed and to turn off the display of the edit line and status bar to maximize the 1-2-3 workspace. You can also hide other worksheet elements, such as worksheet tabs and scroll bars.

Shortcut
Click the Show/Hide Worksheet Elements SmartIcon.

To switch windows
After you choose the Window command from the menu bar, 1-2-3 for Windows lists up to nine open windows at the bottom of the Window menu; a check mark appears next to the active window's name. To make another window active, type the number displayed next to the window name, or click the number in the menu with the mouse. If you have more than nine open windows, you can display all open windows in the Window menu by using the Window More Windows command (which appears only if more than nine windows are open).

To activate a window in the 1-2-3 window, click anywhere inside that window. You also can cycle through the open windows by pressing Ctrl+F6 to activate each window in turn.

To switch among applications
By using the Switch To command on the 1-2-3 Control menu, you can switch to the *Task List*, a Windows Program Manager utility that manages multiple applications. You also can press Ctrl+Esc to access the Task List. For more information about the Task List, refer to your Windows documentation.

> **Tip**
>
> Press Alt+Tab to switch from application to application in Windows. If the application you switch to is reduced to an icon, the icon is restored to a window after you release the Alt key.

1-2-3 for Windows Basics

In 1-2-3 for Windows, a spreadsheet is referred to as a *worksheet* a two-dimensional grid of columns and rows that can be part of a three-dimensional *worksheet file*. Besides working with several worksheets in a file, you can work with several different worksheet files at the same time. You can, for example, link files by writing in one file formulas that refer to cells in another file.

One file can contain up to 256 worksheets, identified by letters followed by colons. Notice that a *worksheet tab* containing the letter *A* appears at the top of the worksheet. A: is the first worksheet, B: is the second, C: is the third, and so on (up to IV:). Each worksheet is made up of 256 columns, labeled A through IV, and 8,192 rows, numbered consecutively. 1-2-3 initially names each tab A, B, C, and so on, but you also can assign names you specify to each worksheet by using the worksheet tabs.

The intersections of rows and columns form *cells*, in which you enter data. Each cell is identified by an address, which consists of a worksheet letter (or worksheet tab name), column letter, and row number.

As you work in the worksheet, 1-2-3 for Windows indicates the *current cell*—the cell in which you can enter data—by a rectangle outline. This rectangle outline is the *cell pointer*. As you enter data in a cell, the data appears directly in the cell as well as in the edit line near the top of the screen. You move the cell pointer by using the direction keys or the mouse.

The 1-2-3 for Windows Screen

The 1-2-3 for Windows screen display is divided into several parts: the control panel, the SmartIcons, the Worksheet window, and the status bar. Together, these parts enable you to work with and display worksheets and graphs.

The following figure shows the 1-2-3 for Windows screen with many of its components numbered. The list that follows indicates the parts of the screen that correspond with the numbers shown in the figure.

8 1-2-3 Release 5 for Windows Quick Reference

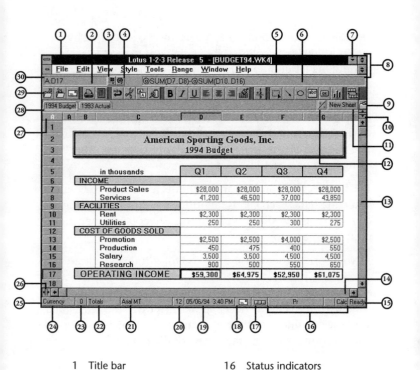

1 Title bar	16 Status indicators
2 Selection indicator	17 SmartIcons selector
3 Navigator	18 Mail button
4 @Function selector	19 Date/Time/Style indicator
5 Menu bar	20 Point-Size selector
6 Contents box	21 Font selector
7 Minimize button	22 Style selector
8 Maximize/Restore buttons	23 Decimal selector
9 Tab button	24 Format selector
10 Horizontal splitter	25 Status bar
11 New Sheet button	26 Vertical splitter
12 Tab scroll buttons	27 Worksheet letter
13 Vertical scroll bar	28 Worksheet tabs
14 Horizontal scroll bar	29 SmartIcons
15 Mode indicator	30 Edit line

The control panel

The *control panel*, which appears at the top of the program window, contains three segments: the *title bar*, which contains the program title, the Control menu box, and the Minimize, Maximize, and Restore buttons; the *menu bar*, which displays the 1-2-3 menus currently available; and the *edit line*, which displays information about the active cell and enables you to edit data in the worksheet. The edit line also includes the navigator and the @function selector. The remainder of this section describes the parts of the edit line.

The edit line's *selection indicator* displays the address of the current selection, which is the selected cell or range. A *cell address* consists of the worksheet letter followed by a colon, the column letter, and the row number. The address of the top left cell in the first worksheet, for example, is A:A1. If you select a range of cells, the selection indicator displays two addresses separated by two periods, which define opposite corners of the range.

The *navigator* accesses a pull-down list that displays all named ranges and objects in the worksheet. (Simply click the navigator to see the list.) If you choose a name from this list while you are working in Edit mode, 1-2-3 places the selected name in the formula you are entering. Otherwise, choosing a name from the navigator list selects (or jumps to) the named range or item.

The *@function selector* displays a list of functions available in 1-2-3. You can use this tool to insert functions into the formula you are currently typing or simply to remind you of 1-2-3's available functions. (For more information on the @function selector, see *Functions* in the Task Reference.)

The right two-thirds of the edit line is the *contents box*. As you enter information into a 1-2-3 for Windows worksheet, the information appears both in the contents box and in the selected cell. If you highlight a cell, the cell's contents appear in the contents box. The difference between the information displayed in the contents box and the information displayed in the cell is that the cell displays the *result* of information that you enter in the worksheet. If you enter a formula, for example, the cell displays the result of the formula—not the formula itself. The contents box, on the other hand, displays the formula exactly as you enter it.

The SmartIcons

SmartIcons are tools that appear in the third line of the 1-2-3 window. Some SmartIcons are shortcuts for menu commands. Other SmartIcons perform specialized actions that you cannot achieve by using menu commands. The SmartIcons you see at the top of the screen are only a few of the many available in 1-2-3 for Windows. (For more information about SmartIcons, see *SmartIcons* in the Task Reference.)

The Worksheet window

1-2-3 for Windows creates special files called *worksheet files*. Each application you create in 1-2-3 uses a worksheet file. After you open a worksheet file in 1-2-3, the file appears in a window called a *Worksheet window*. You can open and view several Worksheet windows at one time and even arrange these windows on-screen.

Each worksheet has its own title bar, which contains a Control menu, Minimize button, and Maximize or Restore button.

The status bar

The *status bar* is the bottom line of the screen. This bar displays information about the attributes of the current cell, such as the font applied to the cell and the number of decimal places used. As you move from cell to cell in the worksheet, the status bar may change to reflect the attributes of each cell as you select that cell.

The status bar also provides a quick method of changing cell attributes. Simply click any formatting attribute displayed in the status bar to display a list of options for that attribute.

The *mode indicator* appears at the far right of the status bar. This indicator tells you what mode 1-2-3 for Windows currently is in and what you can do next. If 1-2-3 for Windows is waiting for your next action, the mode indicator reads Ready. If you change the information in a cell, the mode indicator changes to Edit.

1-2-3 for Windows also displays *status indicators* at the right end of the status bar, immediately to the left of the mode indicator. These status indicators, such as U (for unprotected) and Calc, give you information about the state of the system.

You can remove the status bar from the screen by using the **View** Set **V**iew **P**references command and deselecting the Status **B**ar option.

For more information on using the mouse and keyboard to get around the 1-2-3 for Windows worksheet, see *Navigating the Worksheet* in the Task Reference.

Conventions Used in This Book

To make its information as clear to you as possible, this book follows certain conventions.

If two keys appear joined by a plus sign, such as Shift+Ins, press and hold the first key as you press the second key. If two keys appear together without a plus sign, such as End Home, press and release the first key before you press the second key.

The function keys, F1 through F10, are used for special situations in 1-2-3. In the text, the function-key number and the corresponding function-key name usually are listed together, such as F2 (Edit).

The following special typefaces are used in *1-2-3 Release 5 for Windows Quick Reference*:

Italic	New terms or phrases when initially defined; function and macro-command syntax.
Boldface	Information you are asked to type; letters that you press to access menu and dialog box options (those that appear underscored on-screen)
`Special Type`	Direct quotations of words that appear on-screen or in a figure

If you must select a series of menu options to initiate a command, these options are listed in the order you choose them. File **S**ave, for example, means that you first choose **F**ile and then choose **S**ave.

For easy reference, this book contains text boxes that describe shortcuts for performing operations discussed in a section. If appropriate, a corresponding SmartIcon also appears in the box.

> **Shortcut**
>
> Press Ctrl+S.
>
> or
>
> Click the Save File SmartIcon.

Tip text boxes give optional but useful information for carrying out 1-2-3 tasks.

> **Tip**
>
> If you hold down the Shift key as you draw an ellipse or rectangle, 1-2-3 creates a perfect circle or square. If you press Shift while drawing an arc, 1-2-3 creates a perfect semicircle. Press Shift while drawing a line or arrow and you get a perfectly horizontal, vertical, or 45-degree diagonal line.

Note text boxes provide additional information to assist your work in 1-2-3 for Windows.

> **Note**
>
> The format selector in the status bar displays the format of the current cell. For example, Fixed appears on the format selector when the current cell is formatted with the Fixed format.

A caution text box warns you of a possible pitfall to avoid.

> **Caution**
>
> Usually, deleting rows or columns affects only the current worksheet. If, however, you have grouped together several worksheets with Group mode, when you delete (or add) rows or columns in one worksheet, you delete (or add) the same rows or columns in all the grouped worksheets.

Task Reference

This portion of the *1-2-3 Release 5 for Windows Quick Reference* covers the most fundamental 1-2-3 for Windows tasks and the commands you use to perform them. These tasks are arranged alphabetically for your convenience.

Adding

See *Summing*

Aligning Data

By default, 1-2-3 for Windows aligns labels to the left and values (numbers and formulas) to the right of the cell.

To change the default alignment

1 Choose **S**tyle **W**orksheet Defaults. The Worksheet Defaults dialog box appears.

2 Choose the desired **A**lignment option (Left, Right, or Center) and choose OK.

3 If the file contains multiple worksheets, be sure to click the **G**roup Mode check box to change the default alignment in all the worksheets.

> **Note**
>
> Changing the default alignment has no effect on existing worksheet entries. Any new entries you type into the worksheet, however, conform to the new default alignment style.

Aligning Data

To align data

1 Select the range and then choose **S**tyle **A**lignment. The Alignment dialog box appears.

2 Use the settings in the Horizontal area of the Alignment dialog box to align data horizontally in a cell.

The **G**eneral option left-aligns all labels and right-aligns all numbers in the selected range. The **E**venly Spaced option adds spaces, if necessary, between characters so that label entries fill the selected cell from edge to edge. The **L**eft, **C**enter, and **R**ight options left-align, center-align, and right-align data, respectively.

> **Shortcut**
>
> 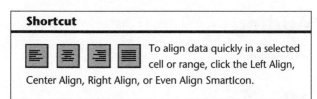 To align data quickly in a selected cell or range, click the Left Align, Center Align, Right Align, or Even Align SmartIcon.

3 Use the settings in the Vertical section of the Alignment dialog box to align data vertically in a cell whose height is bigger than the largest typeface in the current selection.

The **T**op, Ce**n**ter, and **B**ottom options align data to the top, center, or bottom of a cell, respectively.

4 Choose OK.

To align data across multiple columns

When you center or right-align data, the alignment is relative to the column width of the label's cell. If you choose **S**tyle **A**lignment and then select the Acr**o**ss Columns option in the Alignment dialog box, the label is aligned relative to all selected columns. This option can be handy when you want to center a title over a worksheet. When you align across columns, you can specify whether the label is aligned **L**eft, **C**enter, **R**ight, or **E**venly Spaced.

Aligning Data   15

> **Shortcut**
>
> Click the Center Across Columns SmartIcon.

To wrap text in a cell

Choosing the **W**rap Text option in the Alignment dialog box causes 1-2-3 to wrap text at the right edge of the column and carry it to the next line in the cell.

As you type an entry in a cell formatted with the **W**rap Text option, the characters appear across the adjacent columns instead of wrapping because 1-2-3 wraps the text only after you press Enter to confirm the entry in the cell.

> **Note**
>
> You might find it easier to format your worksheet text by placing it in a text block rather than trying to format the data within a cell. See *Text Blocks* for more information.

To change the text orientation

You can alter the direction in which characters appear in a cell or range (the *orientation* of the text) by using the horizontal or vertical option in the Orientation section of the Alignment dialog box. This option can be useful for labeling a worksheet.

> **Shortcut**
>
> To quickly align data at an angle, click the Angle Text SmartIcon.

Approach

1-2-3 Release 5 for Windows includes an interface to Lotus Approach 3.0 for Windows. If you have installed Approach 3.0, you can access new menu options in 1-2-3 for Windows to manage and analyze data in your 1-2-3 database tables. Use the last four options on the **T**ools Data**b**ase menu to:

- Create an Approach Form to view 1-2-3 ranges one record at a time. Data entered or edited in the form dynamically updates the 1-2-3 data.

- Create an Approach Report to organize a 1-2-3 database table for presentation. You can sort and arrange the data as needed and calculate summaries.

- Create an Approach Dynamic Crosstab to summarize categories of data in a 1-2-3 database table, and then embed the resulting crosstab as an icon in the worksheet. Changing the 1-2-3 data causes Approach to update the crosstab data.

- Create Approach Mailing Labels from data in a 1-2-3 database table. Choose from standard label formats or create your own formats.

If you do not have Approach 3.0 installed, an information box is displayed when you select any of these options in 1-2-3 for Windows. A phone number is included for more information on Approach. Click OK to close the box.

Auditing Formulas

When a worksheet is quite large, contains complex formulas, or formulas you're not familiar with (perhaps another user created the worksheet), 1-2-3's audit feature is a useful tool. You can use the audit feature to identify the following:

- All formulas in a worksheet
- Formulas that refer to data in a selected range
- The cells that a formula references
- Formulas with circular references
- Formulas that refer to data in other files (file links)
- Cells that contain a link to data created with another Windows application (DDE links)

To audit formulas

1 Choose **T**ools **A**udit. The Audit dialog box appears.

> **Shortcut**
>
> Click the Audit Cells SmartIcon.

2 Make the desired Audit choices in the Audit area of the Audit dialog box.

3 In the Produce A area of the dialog box, choose how you want 1-2-3 to display the results.

Choose **S**election to highlight all the cells 1-2-3 finds in the active worksheet.

or

Choose **R**eport at Range to list the address of each cell found and its formula in the range you specify. This range must be blank. If you choose a range that contains data, 1-2-3 displays an error message and closes the Audit dialog box, canceling the audit.

18 Auditing Formulas

> **4** Choose an option in the Limit Audit To area.
>
> Choose the Current File option to search for cells in the current worksheet only.
>
> or
>
> Choose the All Files option to search for cells in all worksheets in the active file. You must specify a cell range where 1-2-3 can report the results because 1-2-3 can't display a selection of cells in multiple sheets at once.
>
> **5** Choose OK.

If you chose Selection in step 3, press Ctrl+Enter to move forward from one selected cell to the next; press Ctrl+Shift+Enter to move backwards through the selected cells. Press any arrow key or Esc to deselect the cells.

> **Tip**
>
> 1-2-3 provides a set of SmartIcons especially for sheet auditing. To display these SmartIcons, click the SmartIcons selector in the status bar and choose Sheet Auditing from the list of palettes. Among this set are tools for finding all formulas, finding formula precedents, finding cell dependents, finding file links, and finding DDE links.

Backsolver

You can use the Backsolver, a 1-2-3 Release 5 for Windows analysis tool, to figure out the values a formula needs in order to achieve a certain value. When you use the Backsolver, 1-2-3 changes the value of a variable until the formula dependent on that variable returns the result you want.

To use Backsolver

1 Choose Range Analyze Backsolver. The Backsolver dialog box appears.

2 In the Make Cell text box, specify the cell that contains the formula for which you are seeking a specific result.

3 In the **E**qual to Value text box, enter the number you want the formula to return.

4 In the **B**y Changing Cell(s) text box, enter the cell that contains the variable you want to change to achieve this result.

5 Choose OK.

When you choose OK from the Backsolver dialog box, 1-2-3 for Windows changes the value in the **B**y Changing Cell(s) text box so that the formula in the **M**ake Cell text box returns the amount for **E**qual to Value.

If the Backsolver cannot find a value for **B**y Changing Cell(s) that meets the criteria for the **M**ake Cell formula, 1-2-3 for Windows prompts you with an error message. In this case, you may want to try running the Solver on the problem, and then generate a What-If Limits report to determine reasonable estimates for **B**y Changing Cell(s).

When you use the Backsolver, remember that 1-2-3 for Windows permanently changes the value of **B**y Changing Cell(s). If you plan to use the Backsolver to try a number of different values in a what-if analysis, make sure that you save the worksheet file before you use the Backsolver so that you can return to the original worksheet that contains the starting values.

If you forget to save the worksheet before you use the Backsolver, you can return to the last value in **B**y Changing Cell(s) with the **E**dit **U**ndo command. Note, however, that you return to only the preceding set of values. If you used the Backsolver a number of times, **E**dit **U**ndo cannot return you to the initial values, but returns you to the values before you last chose OK from the Backsolver dialog box.

Bolding

You can add emphasis to data in a selected cell or range by applying boldfacing.

To add boldfacing
1 Highlight the cell or range to which you want to apply boldface.

2 Choose **S**tyle **F**ont & Attributes to open the Font & Attributes dialog box.

3 In the Attributes area, choose the **B**old check box. An X in the check box indicates that bold is selected.

4 Choose OK.

The cell or range is displayed in boldface. Follow the same steps to remove boldface from selected cells, removing the X from the **B**old check box.

Shortcut
Click the Boldface SmartIcon.

Borders

Using the border options, you can apply lines and borders to the worksheet. Borders can be applied to any of the four sides of a cell. By combining borders across many cells, you can outline a range or produce a line across the page.

To apply borders to cells or ranges
1 Highlight the cell or range to which you want to apply borders.

2 Choose **S**tyle **L**ines & Color. The Lines & Color dialog box appears.

> **Shortcut**
>
> Click the Lines & Color SmartIcon.

3 Use the settings in the Border area of the dialog box to draw lines above, below, on the sides of, and around cells in a range. To outline all cells in a selected range (as if they were one object), choose the **O**utline check box.

> **Shortcut**
>
> Click the Add Border SmartIcon.

4 To outline individual cells in the selected range, choose the **A**ll check box. The Sample box shows the effect of your current selections.

5 To further enhance borders, you can choose the **De**signer Frame check box, and then choose a frame style and color from the drop-down lists.

6 Choose OK when you finish selecting border options. The following figure shows different types of borders.

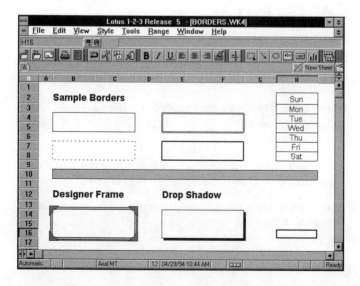

To change or remove borders from cells or ranges

1. Highlight the cell or range containing the border. If you are in doubt as to which cell the border applies, highlight all possible cells. A border that appears on the left side of one cell might actually be applied to the right side of the cell next to it. When in doubt, highlight both cells.

2. Choose **S**tyle **L**ines & Color. The Lines & Color dialog box appears.

3. Use the settings in the Border area of the dialog box to remove all selections, or to change your selections. Note the change in the Sample box.

4. Choose OK.

> **Shortcut**
>
> You can add an outline with a drop shadow to a cell or selected range by clicking the Drop Shadow SmartIcon.

Centering

Centering is an important part of worksheet setup. The following procedures show you how to center data over columns or within a cell.

To center a heading over multiple columns

1. Type a heading at the top of the leftmost column and format the heading the way you want it.

2. Position the cell pointer on the heading cell. Highlight that cell and all the cells above the columns.

3. Choose **S**tyle **A**lignment to open the Alignment dialog box.

4 In the Horizontal area of the dialog box, choose the Center option button and the Across columns check box.

5 Choose OK.

> **Shortcut**
>
> Click the Center Across Columns SmartIcon.

> **Tip**
>
> You can center several headings at once—not just one heading. Suppose that your worksheet displays monthly financial data. Each month requires three columns of data, giving you 36 columns for the year. To center each month heading over its three columns, simply type the month names at the top of the leftmost column of each section. Then highlight the entire row containing the headings and click the Center Across Columns SmartIcon. All the headings will be centered at once.

To center data within a cell

You can center entries if you start by typing the ^ prefix. You can also center data you have already entered in cells:

1 Highlight the cell or range containing the data you want to center.

2 Press Ctrl+E. The data is centered horizontally within each cell you highlighted.

> **Shortcut**
>
> Click the Center Align SmartIcon.

Changing the Working Directory

If you install 1-2-3 for Windows according to the instructions in *Installing 1-2-3 for Windows* in this Task Reference, your worksheet files are stored in the path C:\123R5W\WORK. This directory is called your *working directory*.

Each time you choose **F**ile **O**pen, **F**ile **S**ave, or **F**ile Save **A**s, 1-2-3 automatically assumes you want to open or save files in your working directory.

To change the working directory

1 Choose **T**ools **U**ser Setup. The User Setup dialog box appears.

2 Enter a new path name in the **W**orksheet Directory text box.

3 Click OK to change the working directory for the current and all future work sessions.

Changing the Worksheet Display

See *Worksheet Views*

Charts

You can create 12 types of charts in 1-2-3 Release 5: line, area, bar, pie, XY, high-low-close-open (HLCO), mixed (bar and line), radar, 3D line, 3D area, 3D bar, and 3D pie. You can create a chart quickly from a selected range of data in the worksheet; in a single step, the chart is created and all elements are placed within the chart, including titles, legends, and labels. Charts are updated automatically if any data is changed.

Beyond creating simple charts, 1-2-3 **C**hart commands enable you to enhance and customize your charts. You can use these commands to change the font and color of chart elements, label data points, change the display format of values, create a grid, and change the scaling along the x-axis or y-axis.

After a chart is selected, the main menu displays the **C**hart commands used to create and enhance charts, and the SmartIcon palette changes to display frequently used charting SmartIcons.

Unlike previous versions of 1-2-3, 1-2-3 Release 4 and Release 5 for Windows produce presentation quality charts right in the worksheet and also provide in-place chart editing. Simply click a chart element to select it, and use the **C**hart and **S**tyle commands to add such enhancements as color, designer frames, fonts, and text attributes.

If the worksheet data you want to chart is defined in geographic regions, you may want to use the new mapping tool included with 1-2-3 Release 5 for Windows. See *Mapping*.

The **T**ools **D**raw menu provides additional capabilities for enhancing your worksheet charts. You can add lines, polylines, arrows, rectangles, arcs, ellipses, polygons, and text blocks to your charts. By using the **F**ile **P**rint command, you can print the worksheet data and chart together or you can print a selected chart.

Creating a Chart

To create a chart, you first must open the worksheet file that contains the data you want to plot. To chart information from a worksheet, you must know which data you want to plot and which data you want to use to label the chart.

If you preselect a range of data, you can create a chart quickly and easily. 1-2-3 uses the following rules when displaying charts with preselected ranges:

> *Rule #1:* If a title is anywhere in the first row of the selected range, it becomes the chart title.

Rule #2: If a title is anywhere in the second row, it becomes the chart's subtitle.

Rule #3: Blank rows and columns are ignored completely.

Rule #4: If more rows than columns are in your selected range, 1-2-3 plots the data by column. The first column becomes the x-axis labels, the second column becomes the first data series, the third column becomes the second data series, and so on. The first row after any titles becomes the legend labels.

Rule #5: If more columns than rows are in the selected range, 1-2-3 plots the data by rows. The first row (after any titles or blank rows) becomes the x-axis labels, the second row becomes the first data series, the next row becomes the second data series, and so on. The first column becomes the legend labels.

Rule #6: If you select only numeric data as you create a chart, 1-2-3 follows Rules #4 and #5 to determine how to lay out the chart (by column or by row). 1-2-3 creates a default heading and legend and default axis titles; you can modify this default text by double-clicking the appropriate chart element. You then see the appropriate dialog box (Headings, X-Axis, Y-Axis, or Legend), in which you can change the text. The following section discusses these dialog boxes.

To create a chart

1. Select the range of cells to be charted, including all titles, legend labels, x-axis labels, and the numeric data.

2. Choose **T**ools **C**hart. You see the chart pointer, which looks like a bar chart. The message at the top of the window tells you to click and drag the chart pointer to where you want the chart displayed.

> **Shortcut**
>
> Click the Create Chart SmartIcon.

3 Click the chart pointer at the upper left corner of where you want to place the chart in the worksheet, using the default chart size or by clicking and dragging a box to indicate the specific size of your chart. The default chart is inserted after you click, and the custom-sized chart is inserted after you release the mouse button.

> **Note**
>
> If you do not preselect the range to be charted, the chart dialog box appears when you choose **T**ools **C**hart or click the Create Chart SmartIcon. As prompted in the dialog box, click the range selector button to select the data to chart, or enter the range address in the text box. Click OK, then click the worksheet where you want to place the upper left corner of the chart.

After 1-2-3 creates a chart, the chart is automatically *selected*; you can move, resize, and manipulate it immediately. You can see that the chart is selected because it displays *selection handles*—small black boxes that appear around the border of the chart.

After you create a chart, a new menu, **C**hart, replaces **R**ange in the menu bar. This menu appears in the menu bar only if the chart, or an element in the chart, is selected.

The following figure shows the default chart created for the worksheet range B1..F7. The default chart type is a bar chart. To change the type (to a line, for example, or a pie), use the **C**hart **T**ype command; chart types are discussed in more detail later in this section.

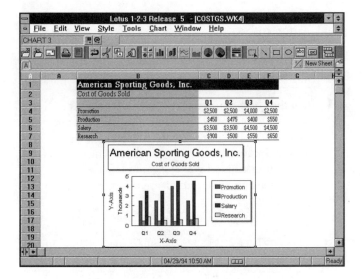

Naming and Finding Charts

1-2-3 names your charts for you as you create them (Chart 1, Chart 2, and so forth). The name of the selected chart (or the last one you selected) appears in the selection indicator on the edit line. To give your charts more descriptive names, use the **C**hart **N**ame command. In the Name dialog box, type the new name in the **C**hart Name text box, or click the current name in the **E**xisting Charts list, and then click the **R**ename button.

To display the chart associated with a name, press F5 (GoTo) or choose **E**dit **G**o To. In the Type of **I**tem list box, choose Chart, and then select the chart name from the list.

Manipulating Chart Elements

One nice aspect of 1-2-3's charts is how malleable they are. You can move, size, delete, or format individual elements on the chart. This flexibility is what makes building charts in 1-2-3 for Windows so easy.

To resize a chart

1 Click the chart's frame so that selection handles appear surrounding the chart.

2 Drag one of these handles until the chart becomes the desired size.

If you drag a corner handle, you change both the height and width of the chart. By dragging a middle handle on the right or left side of the chart, you change just the width. If you drag a middle handle on the top or bottom of the chart, you adjust the height only. To resize the chart proportionally, hold down the Shift key as you drag.

To select a chart object

You must select a chart object before you can copy, delete, rearrange, or move the object; before you can adjust the object's line style or colors; and before you can make other layout changes to the object. You can select one or several objects at a time. To select an object, just click on the object. After an object is selected, selection handles appear around that object.

Shortcut
To select several objects, click the Select Objects SmartIcon, which enables you to "lasso" the objects you want to select.

To deselect all selected items, position the mouse pointer anywhere on the worksheet outside the chart and click. To deselect one item if several items are selected, position the mouse pointer on that item and then press and hold the Shift key as you click the mouse.

To move chart objects
1. Click the chart object you want to move; make sure that selection handles appear only around the desired object, or you may move the wrong object.

2. Place the mouse pointer inside the object and begin dragging; the mouse pointer turns into a hand, a dotted box appears around the object, and the dotted box moves to the new location. (A dotted line appears on lines and arrows.)

3. Release the mouse button after you finish moving the dotted box; the box disappears and the object is moved to the new location in its place.

To resize a chart object
1. Select the object you want to resize, and then place the mouse pointer on one of the object's selection handles. The mouse pointer changes into a four-headed arrow (the mouse pointer for sizing an object).

2. Drag the selection handle with the sizing pointer until outline of the object is the desired size.

3. Release the mouse button.

Resizing a frame works a little differently. As you drag a selection handle, both sides of the box expand or contract. If you drag a right handle to the right, for example, the frame expands on the right *and* on the left, keeping the text inside centered within the frame. (This applies to title, footnote, and legend frames only.)

To delete a chart object
If the chart contains an element you don't want, you can delete that element by selecting the object and pressing the Del key. 1-2-3 enables you to delete the title frame (along with its contents), the legend, the axis titles, the footnote frame (and its contents), x-axis labels, any individual data series, the entire chart, and any objects you added by using

the **T**ools **D**raw commands. You cannot delete the plot, the unit indicator, or the y-axis scale. You cannot delete a frame's contents without deleting the entire frame.

Modifying a Chart

Although 1-2-3's default chart may suit your needs, more often you must change the chart to make it more appropriate for your report or presentation. Sometimes a different type of chart can present the data more effectively; or you simply may want to highlight specific data by exploding a pie slice (that is, removing the slice slightly from the rest of the pie), using a special color, or adding an arrow or other device to catch the reader's attention. This section describes the many ways 1-2-3 for Windows enables you to change and improve a chart.

To specify the chart type and style

By default, 1-2-3 for Windows displays a bar chart when you create a chart. To change the type of chart that 1-2-3 for Windows displays after the default chart appears in the worksheet, follow these steps:

1 Choose **C**hart **T**ype.

> **Shortcut**
>
> Click the Select Chart Type SmartIcon to display the Type dialog box, or click one of the other SmartIcons that directly selects a new chart type (such as the 3D Pie SmartIcon).

2 In the Type dialog box, select one of the chart types.

3 To the right of the Types area, the Type dialog box displays several large buttons showing different styles for the current type of chart. Click one of these chart style buttons.

In the Type dialog box, you also can change the chart from vertical to horizontal orientation, and you can select **I**nclude Table of Values to add a table below the chart that shows the values used to graph each range.

4 Choose OK to confirm your choices and exit the dialog box. 1-2-3 displays the current chart, using the new chart type.

> **Tip**
>
> To save the current chart type, style, and grid settings as a default, select the chart, and then choose **C**hart **S**et Preferred. New charts that you create will use this as the default chart type. To change an existing chart to the new default style, select the chart, then choose **C**hart **U**se Preferred.

To change the orientation of a chart

Chart types that are plotted on an x- and y-axis (line, bar, area, XY, and HLCO) offer an option in the Type dialog box for changing the orientation. **V**ertical is the standard orientation. If you choose H**o**rizontal, the x- and y-axes are swapped.

To specify a custom legend

By default, 1-2-3 for Windows places legend labels in a frame to the right of the chart. The Legend dialog box enables you to specify legend labels by typing the labels directly or by specifying the cell addresses of the labels in the worksheet. To add legend labels, follow these steps:

1 Choose **C**hart **L**egend. The Legend dialog box appears. You also can display this dialog box by double-clicking an existing legend.

2 To specify a legend label, click the appropriate data series letter, and type the label in the **L**egend Entry text box or enter the worksheet cell address that contains the label. (If you enter an address, make sure that you also select the Cell check box.)

3 Repeat the process for each legend label you need to add.

4 Choose OK.

If you prefer to enter legend labels for all ranges concurrently, you can choose [All ranges] in the **S**eries list box. Then, in the **L**egend Entry text box, enter the worksheet range containing the legend labels, or use the range selector to highlight the range.

You also can indicate in the Legend dialog box where to place the legend: **R**ight of plot, **B**elow plot, or **M**anual. **R**ight of plot stacks the labels vertically. **B**elow plot creates a legend with a horizontal orientation; depending on how many labels you have, the legend may wrap onto several lines. You don't need to select the **M**anual option—it's automatically selected after you drag the legend and move it elsewhere within the chart frame.

To customize chart titles and add notes

Choosing the **C**hart **H**eadings command accesses the Headings dialog box, in which you can create two titles and two footnotes for your chart. You use the two Title text boxes to create the title and subtitle; the titles appear centered above the chart, with the first title in larger type above the second title. You use the Note text boxes to add footnotes that appear below the chart.

To enter titles and notes, select the appropriate text box from the Headings dialog box. You can either type the text directly in the text box or select the Cell check box and type the address of the cell that contains the label or number to be used as the title or note.

You can edit titles and notes by choosing the **C**hart **H**eadings command and changing or editing the contents of the text boxes in the Headings dialog box. If you select the entire text box, all its text is highlighted and any new text you type replaces the existing text. To delete text, press Del after the text box is highlighted. Another way to delete a title or note is to select that text in the chart and press Del.

> **Shortcut**
>
> To edit a title or note, double-click the title or note in the chart; the Headings dialog box instantly appears.

By default, titles are centered at the top and notes are left-aligned at the bottom of the chart. By using the Placement options, you can align the titles and notes on the Le**f**t, Ri**g**ht, or Cen**t**er. But you can move titles and notes anywhere on the chart. Simply select the text you want to move by clicking it, and then drag the text block anywhere inside the chart frame. You do not need to select the **M**anual option—it is selected automatically after you manually move a title or note.

To change the axis titles

You specify the axis titles by using the command **C**hart **A**xis. This command enables you to specify and then add titles for the **X**-Axis, **Y**-Axis, and **2**nd Y-Axis. The placement of axis titles depends on whether the chart is horizontally or vertically oriented. In a vertical chart (the default chart orientation), the y-axis title appears left of the y-axis; the x-axis title is centered below the x-axis; and the second y-axis title appears to the right of the second y-axis. By default, 1-2-3 inserts X-Axis and Y-Axis as your axis titles. You can edit the axis titles in the appropriate Axis dialog box by choosing the **C**hart **A**xis command and changing or editing the contents of its text boxes. You also can double-click existing titles to display the appropriate Axis dialog box.

To change the axis scale

As you create a chart, 1-2-3 for Windows sets the *scale*—the minimum to maximum range—of the y-axis based on the smallest and largest numbers in the data range(s) plotted. This default also applies to the second y-axis if you use one. For **X**Y charts, 1-2-3 for Windows also establishes the x-axis scale based on values in the X data range.

To change the axis scale, follow these steps:

1 Choose **C**hart **A**xis **Y**-Axis. The Y-Axis dialog box appears. (The X-Axis and 2nd Y-Axis dialog boxes offer the same options.)

2 Specify different numbers by typing them in the **U**pper limit and Lo**w**er limit text boxes. (Only data that falls between the Lo**w**er and **U**pper limit values is graphed.)

3 Use the **M**ajor interval and Mi**n**or interval text boxes to specify the increments between tick marks.

4 Choose OK.

To return to automatic scaling, deselect all the check boxes in the Scale Manually area; you need not clear out the values or return them to their original values.

To adjust the placement of axis labels

If your axis is crowded with many labels, you can use the **P**lace Label Every [__] Ticks text box in the Y-Axis, X-Axis, or 2nd Y-Axis dialog box to determine how many axis labels appear. If the value in this field is 3, for example, only every third label appears.

You should use this field only if the axis contains values or units of time, where it's obvious what the missing labels are. If the axis contains labels such as product names, however, the chart would not make sense if every other label were missing.

To display a background grid

Grids often make interpreting the data points in charts easier, especially if the data points are far from the x-axis and y-axis labels.

The **C**hart **G**rids command enables you to create horizontal and vertical grid lines for charts that have axes (line, bar, area, XY, HLCO, and mixed charts). The x-axis grid lines extend from tick marks on the x-axis and are perpendicular to the x-axis. The y-axis grid lines extend from y-axis tick marks and are perpendicular to the y-axis. The second y-axis grid lines extend from the tick marks on the second y-axis.

To turn on grid lines, follow these steps:

1 Choose **C**hart **G**rids.

2 Display the drop-down list for **X**-Axis, **Y**-Axis, or **2**nd Y-Axis, and choose from the list's settings: Major Interval, Minor Interval, Both, or None.

The Major intervals are those tick marks that are labeled; the Minor intervals are the smaller tick marks in-between major intervals. The Both setting draws grid lines for major *and* minor intervals, and the None setting eliminates all grid lines.

To add data labels

Knowing the exact value of a data range in a chart can be helpful sometimes. You can label data points in a chart with their corresponding values (called *data labels*) by using the **C**hart **D**ata Labels command. Follow these steps to add data labels:

1 Choose **C**hart **D**ata Labels. The Data Labels dialog box appears.

2 In the **S**eries list box, highlight the series (A, B, C, and so on) for which you want to create data labels, and then specify the range of labels in the **R**ange of Labels text box.

3 Using the **P**lacement drop-down list, you can control whether the data label appears above, centered, below, or to the left or right of the data point.

4 Repeat this process for each series of data labels.

5 Click OK or press Enter. 1-2-3 for Windows displays in the chart the exact value of each data range.

Previewing and Printing Charts

Screen charts are useful for viewing by one or two people, but often you must create printed copies. If you have used earlier versions of 1-2-3, you may notice a major change in the way charts are printed in 1-2-3 Release 5 for Windows. Instead of using a separate PrintGraph program, you now can preview and print charts by using 1-2-3 for Windows' **F**ile **P**rint command.

To print a chart

1 Select any element on the chart.

2 Choose **F**ile **P**rint. The Print dialog box appears with that chart's name entered in the Selected Chart box.

3 Click OK, or press Enter. The chart prints at the same size it appears in the worksheet.

> **Note**
>
> If you want the chart to appear in the worksheet at its current size, but print in full-page size, you can use the Si**z**e option in the Page Setup dialog box. (Choose **F**ile Pa**g**e Setup to access this dialog box.)

To preview a chart

You can preview a chart before you print it. Previewing can save you time and paper, enabling you to make all adjustments and changes before you print. To preview a chart, choose the **F**ile Print Pre**v**iew command or select the **P**review button in the Print dialog box.

> **Shortcut**
>
> Click the Preview SmartIcon.

When you add a chart to a worksheet, you specify the size of the chart and the location at which it appears on the page. By previewing the report, you can determine how the chart fits on the printed page. You then can decide whether you should use one of the Size options in the Page Setup dialog box.

Clearing Cells and Ranges

See *Erasing Cells and Ranges*

Clip Art

You may want to further enhance your charts and worksheets by using *clip art* (simple graphic drawings). Although 1-2-3 for Windows does not provide a specific command for importing graphics files, you can easily bring in clip art by using the Windows Clipboard. Simply copy the graphic to the Clipboard, and use the Edit Paste command in 1-2-3. Before pasting clip art into a worksheet, select a range of cells; the graphic is pasted into this range. (If you don't preselect a range, the graphic is pasted into a single cell.) You then can enlarge the graphic by dragging one of its selection handles.

To place a piece of clip art onto a chart, you first must paste it into a worksheet range. You then can drag the graphic onto your chart and resize it as necessary. The graphic automatically has an outline around it. To remove this outline, choose the Style Lines & Color command and choose None for the Line Style.

Where does clip art come from? Many drawing programs (such as CorelDRAW!) come with a collection of images that you can use in other programs. You also can purchase packages of clip art from companies such as Masterclip Graphics,

3G Graphics, TMaker, and Image Club. Lotus Development offers its own clip art package, called SmartPics. For more information on how you can obtain Lotus SmartPics for Windows, call Lotus Selects at 1-800-635-6887.

> **Tip**
>
> You can use the **E**dit Insert **O**bject command to import objects directly to the chart or worksheet from some applications—for example, SmartPics. In the Insert Object dialog box, select Lotus SmartPics Image from the **O**bject type list box, and then click OK. The SmartPics application starts. Locate the clip art image, then double-click it to place it directly into the 1-2-3 worksheet, where it then can be resized and placed.

Clipboard

All Windows applications share a common Clipboard that can transfer virtually anything from one Windows application to another. In this book, you have already learned how to use the Windows Clipboard to copy and paste 1-2-3 data between cells or between worksheets. The same principle lets you copy and paste information between different applications.

When you use the Clipboard to copy and paste work from one application to another, you end up with two unrelated objects: the original in the application in which it was made, and the duplicate in another application, with no ties that link it to the original. If you modify the original, the duplicate remains unchanged.

To perform a simple copy and paste

1 Select the item to be copied in the first application.

2 Choose **E**dit **C**opy from that application to copy the item to the Windows Clipboard.

3 Switch to the second application.

4 Choose **E**dit **P**aste to paste the item from the Windows Clipboard into the second application.

Closing Files

Closing a file is not the same as saving a file. *Closing* a file removes the file from the screen and from memory without necessarily saving it. *Saving* a file saves the changes and keeps the file open.

To close a file

When you finish working with a file, choose **F**ile **C**lose to remove the current file from the screen and from the list of open files on the **W**indow menu. If you have made unsaved changes to the file when you select **F**ile **C**lose, 1-2-3 displays a warning that allows you to save the most recent changes. Choose **Y**es to save changes, **N**o to close the file without saving changes, or **C**ancel to return to working on the file.

Shortcut
Click the Close Window SmartIcon.

If you are working with many open files at one time, closing a file that you are finished working with is a good idea. The more files open at a time, the less available memory you have. Closing a file frees up memory, enabling you to work more efficiently with the files that remain open.

You can use the **F**ile E**x**it command to exit the 1-2-3 program; this command doesn't automatically close all open files, however. If you choose **F**ile E**x**it while files are still open, 1-2-3 gives you the opportunity to save each open file before exiting the program.

> **Shortcut**
>
> Click the End 1-2-3 Session SmartIcon.

Colors

See *Lines and Colors*

Column Widths

When you start a new worksheet, the column width of all the columns is nine characters. This column width number *approximates* the number of characters that can be displayed. The actual display depends on the typeface and point size of the cell and the individual characters in the cell's data.

You may need to change the width of a column or the height of a row to display your data properly. If columns are too narrow, asterisks appear instead of numbers in the cells, and labels are truncated if the adjacent cell to the right contains data. If columns are too wide, you may not be able to see enough data on-screen or print enough data on one page.

Whether a number can fit into a cell depends on both the column width and the format of the number. Some negative numbers display with parentheses, which take two extra characters. If a number displays as a row of asterisks, you need to change the column width, the format, or both.

You can change the width of all the columns in the worksheet or the width of individual columns.

To change the default width

You can change the column width for the entire worksheet by using the **S**tyle **W**orksheet Defaults command. In the Worksheet Defaults dialog box, specify the new column width, from 1 to 240 characters, in the Column **W**idth text box and choose OK or press Enter. This new setting is applied as the default column width for the current worksheet; any columns you insert will use the new width. The program also immediately adjusts the widths of all columns in the worksheet—except those set earlier to individual widths.

To change individual column widths

You can change the width of one or more columns by using the keyboard and the **S**tyle **C**olumn Width command. Alternatively, you can use the mouse to change the width of one or more columns.

To change the width of an individual column, use these steps for the keyboard:

1 Select a cell or range in the column you want to change.

2 Choose **S**tyle **C**olumn Width. The Column Width dialog box appears.

3 Enter the new column width, from 1 to 240 characters, in the **S**et Width To text box.

4 Choose OK.

If you didn't preselect the column you want to change, you can specify the column or columns in the **C**olumn(s) text box.

1-2-3 shows the column width in the date/time/style indicator in the status bar. If your indicator shows the date and time, click it once to display the column width and row height.

You can change the width of several columns by selecting a range that includes the columns before you issue the command. All columns represented in the range will be affected when you use the **S**tyle **C**olumn Width command.

To change the width of an individual column, use these steps for the mouse:

1. Move the mouse pointer to the column border (to the right of the column letter in the worksheet frame) until the mouse pointer changes to a double arrow pointing horizontally.

2. Press and hold down the left mouse button.

3. Drag the column border left or right to its new position and release the mouse button.

When you use the mouse to change the width of a column, 1-2-3 for Windows displays a solid vertical line that moves with the mouse pointer and shows you the position of the new column border. You can change several columns at once with the mouse by clicking on the first column's heading (for example, the letter A for column A) and dragging to highlight additional columns. Next, adjust the width of any one of the highlighted columns. All highlighted columns comply with your changes.

To fit the column width to the data

A useful feature of 1-2-3 for Windows is the capacity to set a column width to match the data contained in the column. Using this feature prevents you from having to guess at what column width you need to accommodate long entries. You can adjust the width to fit by using one of three methods:

- Double-click the right border of the column heading.

- Choose **S**tyle **C**olumn Width, specify **F**it Widest Entry in the Column Width dialog box, specify the range in the **C**olumn text box (if you didn't preselect the range), and then choose OK or press Enter.

Shortcut

 Click the column heading to highlight the column, and then click the Size Column SmartIcon.

For any of these methods, 1-2-3 for Windows immediately adjusts the column width to match the longest entry.

To restore the default width

To reset an individual column width to the worksheet default, select a cell in the column and choose **R**eset to Worksheet Default in the Column Width dialog box (accessed by choosing **S**tyle **C**olumn Width). Alternatively, you can choose **R**eset and then specify the column(s) you want to reset in the **C**olumn(s) text box.

To change column widths in Group mode

Individual column widths and global column widths can apply to several worksheets if you first group them together with Group mode. When you group worksheets together, any formatting change (such as setting column widths) that you make to one worksheet in the group affects all worksheets in that group.

Combining Values from Separate Files

1-2-3 lets you use values from one file to replace values, add to values, or subtract from values in the current worksheet file, beginning at the current cell.

To combine values from separate files

1 Open the source file by using the **F**ile **O**pen command.

 The source file must already have been saved to disk before it can be combined with another file. If the file is already open and has not yet been saved, choose **F**ile Save **A**s, and then name the file.

2 Choose **F**ile **O**pen to open the file that will contain the combined values. This file will be called the *current* file in the steps that follow.

 The current file can be Untitled, the unnamed start-up worksheet.

Combing Values from Separate Files   **45**

3 Choose **W**indow **T**ile to display the files side by side. Make sure that the current file is active.

4 In the current file, place the cell pointer in the cell where you want values to be copied. (If you are combining a range in the source file with the current file, place the cell pointer in the current file at the position where you want the source cells to begin. Otherwise, place the cell pointer in cell A1.)

5 Choose **F**ile **O**pen. In the Open File dialog box, select the source file, and then click the **C**ombine button. 1-2-3 displays the Combine 1-2-3 File dialog box. The From file field lists the name of the source file.

6 Choose **E**ntire file or **R**ange.

7 Choose Replace **V**alues, **A**dd to Values, or **S**ubtract from Values, and then click OK. 1-2-3 changes the values in the current worksheet file immediately, beginning at the location of the current cell.

To combine values from additional source files, repeat these steps to open and combine each additional file. In each case, you can choose to replace, add to, or subtract from the values in the current file.

In the Combine 1-2-3 File dialog box, the **A**dd to Values option adds the value of a cell in the source file to the value of the corresponding cell in the current file. If the incoming value is combined with a blank cell, the cell takes the value of the number. If the incoming value is combined with a label or formula, 1-2-3 for Windows ignores the incoming value and keeps the label or formula.

The **S**ubtract from Values option subtracts the value of a cell in the source file from the value of the corresponding cell in the current file. If the incoming value is combined with a blank cell, 1-2-3 for Windows subtracts the incoming value from zero. If the incoming value is combined with a label or formula, 1-2-3 for Windows ignores the incoming value and keeps the label or formula.

Copying Data

In a copy operation, just as in a move operation, the data being moved or copied is called the *source* and the location to which you are moving the data is called the *target* or *destination*. When you copy data, 1-2-3 for Windows leaves the source data in its original location and places a copy of the data in the target location. Copied data includes the same labels and values—as well as the same formats, fonts, colors, protection status, and borders—as the original data. You do not, however, copy the column width or row height. You can use **E**dit **C**opy with **E**dit Paste **S**pecial to copy some of the properties or types of data.

If the destination range contains data, 1-2-3 replaces that data with the data you copy unless the destination cells are protected. To help prevent overwriting existing data, be sure to specify a destination large enough to contain the source data.

Remember that you can use the **E**dit **U**ndo command to correct a mistake in copying a range.

Shortcut
Press Ctrl+Z (Undo). or Click the Undo SmartIcon.

Whenever you need to copy data, the drag-and-drop technique is probably the right choice. The **E**dit **C**opy command is primarily for copying data to and from other applications or when you want to copy the same data to a number of different locations. It is also helpful for copying data across large areas of the worksheet where dragging might be more tedious.

To copy with drag-and-drop

1 Highlight the cell or range you want to copy.

2 Next, move the mouse pointer to any edge of the selection (until the mouse pointer changes to a hand).

3 Hold the Ctrl key down as you click and drag the selection to its new location. When you reach the destination, release the mouse and the Ctrl key.

1-2-3 for Windows copies the data to the new location without changing the original.

To drag-and-drop across the worksheet

You may want to copy the data to a distant area in the worksheet, or to a separate sheet in the worksheet. You can still use drag-and-drop if you first window the two areas.

1 Choose **V**iew **S**plit. The sheet splits into two windows.

2 In one of the windows, scroll to display the range to be copied.

3 In the other window, click a sheet tab or the New Sheet button if the data is to be copied to another sheet. Scroll to the area of the sheet where the data will be copied.

4 Highlight the cell or range you want to copy.

5 Next, move the mouse pointer to any edge of the selection (until the mouse pointer changes to a hand).

6 Hold the Ctrl key down as you click and drag the selection to its new location in the other window. When you reach the destination, release the mouse and the Ctrl key.

If you try to drop the range in an area that already has data, 1-2-3 for Windows asks you if it is OK to replace the data. Choose OK to replace the data, or Cancel to avoid copying over the data.

To drag-and-drop across files

1 Open the source file and the file to which you want to copy data, the destination file.

2 Choose **W**indow **T**ile to display the files side by side. Scroll each window to make the source and destination areas visible.

3 Highlight the cell or range you want to copy.

4 Next, move the mouse pointer to any edge of the selection (until the mouse pointer changes to a hand).

5 Click and drag the selection to its new location in the other window. When you reach the destination, release the mouse button.

It is not necessary to hold down the Ctrl key to drag-and-drop to another file. The range remains in the original file.

To copy with Copy and Paste

The **E**dit **C**opy command uses the Clipboard to copy data. No dialog box appears; 1-2-3 for Windows just copies the source data to the Clipboard. To complete the copying action, you must paste the source data with the **E**dit **P**aste command. In addition to copying data between 1-2-3 for Windows files, you also can copy data from and to other Windows applications with this method.

To use the Clipboard to copy data, follow these steps:

1 Highlight the range or cell you want to copy.

2 Choose **E**dit **C**opy.

Shortcut
Press Ctrl+Ins or Ctrl+C.
or
Click the Copy SmartIcon.

3 Move the cell pointer to the first cell of the destination range.

4 Choose **E**dit **P**aste.

Shortcut
Press Enter or Shift+Ins or Ctrl+V.
or
Click the Paste SmartIcon.

To copy a formula with relative addressing

The real power of copying becomes evident when you copy formulas. When you copy a formula, 1-2-3 for Windows adjusts the copied formula so that its cell references are in the same relative location as in the original formula. This process, called *relative addressing*, is the default method of copying formulas.

The best way to understand relative addressing is to understand how 1-2-3 for Windows stores addresses in formulas. The formula @SUM(C2..C5) means that you sum the contents of all the cells in the range from cell C2 to cell C5, but that is not the way 1-2-3 for Windows stores this formula. If this formula is in cell C7, for example, 1-2-3 for Windows reads the formula as "sum the contents of all the cells in the range from the cell five rows above this cell to the cell two rows above this cell." When you copy this formula from cell C7 to cell D7, 1-2-3 for Windows uses the same relative formula but displays it as @SUM(D2..D5).

To copy a formula with absolute addressing

In most cases, when you copy a formula, you want the addresses adjusted automatically. Sometimes, however, you do not want some addresses to be adjusted. In this case, you need to use *absolute addressing*.

To specify an absolute address, type a dollar sign (**$**) before each part of the address you want to remain absolutely the same. For example, if you copy the formula +C7/$F$7 in cell C9 to cell D9, the formula becomes +D7/$F$7.

You can specify an absolute address without typing dollar signs. After you type the address, just press F4 (Abs); the address changes to absolute. 1-2-3 for Windows automatically adds the dollar signs to the address.

You also can use F4 (Abs) while pointing to addresses in a formula. As you point to a cell to include it in a formula, press F4 (Abs) to make the address absolute. If you make an error and forget to make an address absolute, just press F2 (Edit) to switch to Edit mode, move the cursor in the contents box to the address you want to make absolute, and press F4 (Abs).

If you want to change an absolute reference (with dollar signs) back to a relative reference, press Edit (F2), move the cursor to the reference, and then press F4 as many times as necessary until there are no dollar signs. Press Enter to reenter the formula.

To copy a formula with mixed addressing

In some cases, you must use formulas with a mix of absolute and relative references if you want the formula to copy correctly. The example presented in this section shows you how to keep a row reference absolute while letting the column reference change during the copy.

If you copy the formula +B3*(1+C$1) in cell C3 down one row to cell C4, the formula becomes +B4*(1+C$1). The relative address B3 becomes B4, but the mixed address C$1 is unchanged. When you copy this formula to cell D3, the formula becomes +C3*(1+D$1). The relative address B3 becomes C3, and the mixed address C$1 becomes D$1.

To make an address mixed without typing the dollar signs, use F4 (Abs). The first time you press F4, the address becomes absolute. If you continue to press F4, the address cycles through all the possible mixed addresses and returns to relative. The following table is a complete list of relative, absolute, and mixed addresses.

Address	Status
$A:$D$1	Completely absolute
$A:D$1	Absolute worksheet and row
$A:$D1	Absolute worksheet and column
$A:D1	Absolute worksheet
A:$D$1	Absolute column and row
A:D$1	Absolute row
A:$D1	Absolute column
A:D1	Returned to relative

When you work with multiple worksheets, be careful with absolute and mixed addresses. When you first press F4, the first absolute and mixed addresses make the worksheet letter absolute.

To copy one cell to a range
When copying and pasting, you can copy a single cell to a range of cells by highlighting the destination range before using the **E**dit **P**aste command.

To copy styles with Paste Special
When you use the **E**dit **C**opy command, 1-2-3 for Windows copies all aspects of the cell or range—including the underlying values and the formats. If you want to paste only one aspect of the copied data, use the **E**dit Paste **S**pecial command instead of **E**dit **P**aste. This enables you to copy just the formatting of cells, instead of data and formats.

Copying Data

> **Shortcut**
>
> You can copy a cell's styles quickly by selecting the cell containing the styles you want to copy and then choosing the **S**tyle Fas**t** Format command or clicking the Fast Format SmartIcon. The mouse pointer changes to a paint brush. Click the cell to which you want to copy the formats (or click-and-drag across a cell range) and release the mouse button.

You can also choose the **F**ormulas As Values option in the Paste Special dialog box to convert formulas into their underlying values when pasting. 1-2-3 for Windows does not recalculate formulas before it converts the formulas to values. If recalculation is set to manual or if the Calc indicator appears in the status bar, press F9 (Calc) or click the Calc button in the status bar.

To transpose ranges

The **R**ange **T**ranspose command provides another way to copy data. This operation converts rows to columns or columns to rows and changes formulas to values at the same time. The Transpose dialog box provides the **F**rom and **T**o options.

The **R**ange **T**ranspose command copies formats, fonts, colors, and shading but does not copy shadow boxes or border lines.

Range **T**ranspose doesn't recalculate the worksheet before transposing the range, so you need to recalculate the worksheet before issuing this command. If you transpose a range without recalculating, you can freeze incorrect values.

> **Shortcut**
>
> Click the Transpose Data SmartIcon.

Creating Files

When you start 1-2-3, the Welcome dialog box is presented (unless you have disabled this feature). If you choose the option to create a new worksheet file, the New File dialog box appears. If you want to create additional new files during the same work session, choose **File New**, which also displays the New File dialog box. Any files that are open when you choose **File New** remain open afterward. The new file becomes an open file and is listed on the **W**indow menu. 1-2-3 assigns temporary file names to new files you create.

Shortcut
Click the Create File SmartIcon.

To create a new worksheet file

1 Choose **File New**, or when first starting 1-2-3, select the **C**reate a New Worksheet option button in the Welcome dialog box. The New File dialog box is displayed.

2 To create a new file based on a plain worksheet, select the **C**reate a Plain Worksheet check box.

Shortcut
Click the Quick New File SmartIcon.

Or, if you want to base the new file on a SmartMaster template, highlight a selection in the Create a Worksheet By Selecting a **S**martMaster list box. A description is shown in the Comments box, and the file name is shown.

54 Creating Files

The 1-2-3 default SmartMasters are stored in the \123R5W\MASTERS directory. Choose the **B**rowse button if your SmartMaster is stored in another directory. For more information on SmartMasters, see *SmartMasters*.

3 Choose OK. 1-2-3 creates a new worksheet with a default file name, such as FILE0001.WK4.

To record or display file information

When you create a new worksheet file, you may want to record more information about the purpose of the file, especially if the file is shared with others.

1 Choose **F**ile **D**oc Info. The Doc Info dialog box appears. The file name and author appear at the top of the dialog box and cannot be revised.

2 In the **T**itle text box, enter a title for the file.

3 In the **S**ubject text box, enter a subject.

4 In the **K**eywords text box, enter keywords, separated by commas.

5 In the **C**omments text box, enter any comments. These comments are displayed when you select this file in the Open File, Save As, and New File dialog boxes.

6 In the **R**evisions text box, enter notes about revisions.

7 Click OK.

Other statistics appear at the bottom of the Doc Info dialog box, including date and time created and last revised, person revised by and total revisions, editing time, and number and size of worksheets. The information in the Doc Info dialog box can be passed to Lotus Notes, if you have installed Notes. See *Notes*.

Cross Tabulation

See *Database Management: Creating Crosstabs and Aggregates*

Data Entry

See *Entering Data*

Database Management

1-2-3 Release 5 for Windows provides true database management commands and functions, enabling you to sort, query, extract, and perform analysis on data and even access and manipulate data from an external database. The 1-2-3 for Windows database features are easy to use because they are integrated with the worksheet and chart functions. The commands you use to add, modify, and delete items in a database are the same ones you already have used to manipulate cells or groups of cells in a worksheet.

Release 5 provides a graphical approach to extracting information from a database, relying on dialog boxes to guide you through the process. This "Query by Box" technology enables you to use drop-down menus and dialog boxes to quickly and easily build the criteria for your databases.

1-2-3 for Windows also provides many advanced database features, including some of the relational enhancements and larger databases of such products as dBASE.

1-2-3 Release 5 for Windows includes an interface to Lotus Approach 3.0 for Windows, which enables you to manage and analyze data in your 1-2-3 database tables. See *Approach* for a description of the main features.

Defining a Database

A *database* is a collection of related information—data organized so that you can list, sort, or search it. The list of data may contain any kind of information, from addresses to tax-deductible expenditures.

In 1-2-3 for Windows, the word *database* means a range of cells that spans at least one column and more than one row. Because a database actually is a list, the manner in which database data is organized sets it apart from data in ordinary cells. Just as a list must be organized to be useful, a database must be organized to permit access to the information it contains.

Databases are made up of fields and records. A *field*, or single data item, is the smallest unit in a database. To develop a database of companies with which you do business, for example, you can include the following fields for each company:

Name

Address

City

State

ZIP

Phone

A *record* is a set of associated fields—that is, the accumulation of all data about one company forms one record. The six fields in the preceding paragraph represent one record.

A database must be set up so that you can access the information it contains. Retrieval of information usually involves key fields. A database *key field* is any field on which you base a list, sort, or search operation. You can use ZIP, for example, as a key field to sort the data in the company database and to assign contact representatives to specific geographic areas.

A 1-2-3 for Windows database resides in the worksheet's row-and-column format. The following figure shows the general organization of a 1-2-3 for Windows database. Labels, or *field names*, that describe the data items appear as column headings in row 1. Information about each specific data item (a field) is entered in a cell in the appropriate column. The following figure illustrates the organization of a 1-2-3 for Windows database.

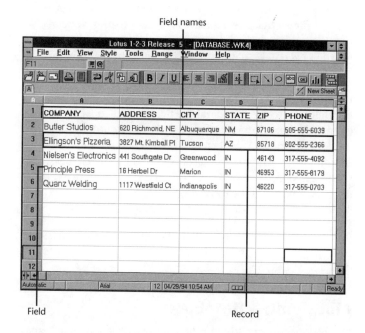

Field names

Field

Record

You use both the **T**ools Data**b**ase and **Q**uery menu commands as you work with 1-2-3 for Windows databases. You access these commands from the 1-2-3 for Windows main menu (the **Q**uery menu appears in place of the **R**ange menu when a *query table*—a range where you can manipulate database information—is selected). The **T**ools Data**b**ase commands create new query tables, access records in a database, and control connections to external database files. The Query commands enable you to manipulate data in query tables and to update information in the database.

Creating a Database

You can create a database as a new worksheet file or as part of an existing file. If you decide to build a database in an existing worksheet, choose an area of the worksheet that you do not need for any other purpose. This area should be large enough to accommodate the number of records that you plan to enter during the current session and in the future.

A better idea, however, is to add another worksheet to the current file so that the database and the existing worksheet don't interfere with one another. To add another worksheet for the new database, use the **E**dit **I**nsert **S**heet command.

The mechanics of entering database contents are simple; the most critical step in creating a useful database is choosing the fields correctly. The database field names must be labels, even if they are numeric labels ('1, '2, and so on). All field names must be in a single row, and field names must be unique. Do not leave any blank columns in the database. Use the **S**tyle **A**lignment options to adjust the appearance if the database appears to be too crowded.

After you enter field names, you can add records to the database. To enter the first record, move the cell pointer to the row directly below the field-name row and then enter the data across the row.

Modifying a Database

You use the same commands to add, modify, and delete items in a database that you already have used to manipulate cells or groups of cells in a worksheet. Commands for moving cells, formatting cells, and displaying the contents of worksheets also work the same in database and worksheet applications.

To modify a database

To add and delete records in a database, you use the same commands that you use to insert and delete rows—**E**dit **I**nsert **R**ow and **E**dit **D**elete **R**ow. If you want to remove only inactive records, consider first using the **T**ools Data**b**ase **N**ew Query command to store the extracted inactive records in a separate query table. You also can use the **T**ools Data**b**ase **D**elete Records command to remove database records. (The **T**ools Data**b**ase commands are discussed later in this section.)

To add a new field to a database, place the cell pointer anywhere in the column to the right of the newly inserted column and then issue the **E**dit **I**nsert **C**olumn command. You then can fill the field with the appropriate values for each record.

To delete a field, position the cell pointer anywhere in the column that you want to remove and then choose the **E**dit **D**elete **C**olumn command.

You modify fields in a database the same way that you modify the contents of cells. You change cell contents either by retyping the cell entry or by pressing F2 (Edit) and then editing the entry.

Using Query Tables

Although you can work with a 1-2-3 for Windows database the way you work with any other range, 1-2-3 for Windows provides a much easier method of working with databases: using query tables. *Query tables* are special areas in a worksheet that simplify the selecting, sorting, and updating of database records. You can decide whether to view all or only some of the fields; you can choose selected groups of records to include in the query table; and you can easily perform summary calculations on selected records.

Because query tables overwrite existing worksheet data, you should create a new worksheet for each query table you use.

To create a query table

1 Highlight the database range, and choose **T**ools Data**b**ase **N**ew Query. The New Query dialog box appears.

> **Shortcut**
>
> Click the Query Table SmartIcon.

2 In the Select Location for New **Q**uery Table text box, type a location for the query table (use a new worksheet if possible).

3 Choose OK to confirm your dialog-box choices and create the query table. A border around the query table indicates that you can change the size of the query table to display more data.

> **Shortcut**
>
> Click the Show All Query Table Records SmartIcon to expand the query table.

You click the border of a query table to select the entire table. After a query table is selected, the **R**ange menu is replaced by the **Q**uery menu, and several standard SmartIcons are replaced by SmartIcons that pertain specifically to query tables. These changes make using a query table even easier.

Sorting Database Records

Although you can use the **R**ange **S**ort command to sort the database range just like any other 1-2-3 for Windows range, this command works only in a worksheet database, not in an external database. You also may become confused if you use the **R**ange **S**ort command to sort a database. You may inadvertently sort the field names into the records, for example, or accidentally destroy the database's integrity by neglecting to include all the fields.

The **Q**uery **S**ort command solves these problems and offers additional benefits. If you use **Q**uery **S**ort, 1-2-3 for Windows displays the sorted records in the query table. You can try several different sort orders without affecting the original database. If you find a sort order that you like, you can apply the new order to the database. If you decide not to apply the changes, the database remains untouched.

To sort records, you must specify the keys to use for the sort. The field with the highest precedence is the first key, the field with the next-highest precedence is the second key, and so on. You can use up to 255 keys in a sort, but you always must set the first key.

To sort records using a single key

1 Click the border of the query table to select it.

2 Choose **Q**uery **S**ort. The Sort dialog box appears.

3 In the drop-down **S**ort By list, select a field name.

4 Choose either **A**scending or **D**escending sort order.

Shortcut
Click the Ascending Sort or Descending Sort SmartIcon.

5 Choose OK.

Sometimes, sorting on a single key does not sort the records in exactly the order you need. In such a case, you can use multiple sort keys to specify additional sorting conditions.

To sort records using multiple keys

1 Click the border of the query table to select it.

2 Choose **Q**uery **S**ort. The Sort dialog box appears.

3 In the drop-down **S**ort By list, select a field name.

4 Choose either **A**scending or **D**escending sort order.

62 Database Management

> **Shortcut**
>
> [icons] Click the Ascending Sort or Descending Sort SmartIcon.

5 Click the Add **K**ey button, and repeat steps 2 and 3 to specify additional sort keys.

6 Choose OK.

Searching for Records

In addition to searching for an exact match of a single label field, 1-2-3 for Windows enables you to conduct a wide variety of record searches: exact matches of numeric fields; partial matches of field contents; searches for fields that meet all of several conditions; and searches for fields that meet either one condition or another.

You can specify selection criteria either as you create a new query table or after an existing query table is selected.

The following table shows how you can use wild cards in search operations.

Enter	To Find
N?	Any two-character label starting with the letter *N* (NC, NJ, and so on)
BO?L?	A five-character label (BOWLE) but not a shorter label (BOWL)
BO?L*	A four-or-more-character label (BOWLE, BOWL, BOELING, and so on)
SAN*	A three-or-more-character label starting with SAN and followed by any number of characters (SANTA BARBARA and SAN DIEGO)
SAN *	A four-or-more-character label starting with SAN, followed by a space, and then followed by any number of characters (SAN DIEGO, but not SANTA BARBARA)

Use the ? and * wild cards if you are unsure of the spelling or if you need to match several slightly different records.

To set up criteria formulas that query numeric or label fields in the database, you can use the following relational operators:

Operator	Meaning
>	Greater than
>=	Greater than or equal to
<	Less than
<=	Less than or equal to
=	Equal to
<>	Not equal to

To specify selection criteria

1 Choose **T**ools Data**b**ase **N**ew Query Set **C**riteria (for a new query table) or **Q**uery Set **C**riteria (for an existing query table). The Set Criteria dialog box appears.

> **Shortcut**
>
> 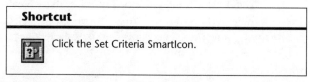 Click the Set Criteria SmartIcon.

2 Specify a criterion by choosing one item each from the **F**ield list, the Op**e**rator list, and the **V**alue list.

To determine which companies in a company database are in Indiana, for example, choose STATE in the **F**ield list, = in the Op**e**rator list, and IN in the **V**alue list.

3 Choose OK to confirm your selection. The query table now contains only the records that match the selection criteria.

64 Database Management

To highlight specified records

1 Highlight the database range, and choose **T**ools Data**b**ase **F**ind Records. The Find Records dialog box appears.

2 Specify a criterion by choosing one item each from the Field list, the Op**e**rator list, and the **V**alue list.

3 Choose OK to confirm your selection. Each record in the database that meets the conditions specified in the Find Records dialog box is highlighted.

Because the highlighted records are selected, you can easily copy, move, or delete them. The **T**ools Data**b**ase **F**ind Records command has limited use, however, especially in a large database. If you want to modify information in the selected records, using a query table is easier.

To delete specified records

You can use the **E**dit **D**elete **R**ow command to remove rows from a worksheet or database. A fast alternative is to use the **T**ools Data**b**ase Delete Records command to remove unwanted records from your database files.

Before you issue the **T**ools Data**b**ase **D**elete Records command, use **T**ools Data**b**ase **F**ind Records or **T**ools Data**b**ase **N**ew Query to make certain that the criterion you specify selects the correct group of records. The **T**ools Data**b**ase **D**elete Records command does not prompt for confirmation before deleting records.

Suppose that you want to remove all records with entries in the STATE field that begin with the letter *N*. Follow these steps:

1 Highlight the database range.

2 Choose **T**ools Data**b**ase **D**elete Records.

3 Specify the selection criterion as **STATE=N***.

4 Choose OK.

The specified records are deleted from the database. 1-2-3 for Windows packs the remaining records together and adjusts the database range.

To modify records

In addition to finding and deleting database records, you probably will want to modify records. In worksheet databases, you can modify records directly in the database range, but using a query table is safer. The query-table procedure also enables you to modify records in external databases.

To use a query table to modify records, follow these steps:

1 Retrieve the database containing the records that you want to modify.

2 Edit the records directly in the query table, either by making the changes manually or by using **E**dit **F**ind & Replace.

3 Highlight the query table, and choose **Q**uery **U**pdate Database Table.

If **Q**uery **U**pdate Database Table is dimmed, choose **Q**uery **S**et **O**ptions **A**llow Updates to Source Table.

Creating Crosstabs and Aggregates

Crosstabs summarize data by showing how two factors influence a third factor. For example, a database can track the amount of each sale for three different salespersons selling three different categories of products. A cross tabulation shows summary information you can use to analyze how well each salesperson is doing.

An *aggregate* is a variation of a cross tabulation. Instead of being placed in a separate cross-tabulation table, the data in an aggregate analysis is placed in a column of a query table.

To create a crosstab

1. Choose **T**ools Data**b**ase Cross**t**ab. The Crosstab dialog box appears.

Shortcut
Click the Crosstab SmartIcon.

2. Specify the database range you want to analyze. This range *must* include at least three columns and two rows.

3. Select Continue. The Crosstab Heading Options dialog box appears.

4. Specify which database field contains the values you want to display down the left side of the cross-tabulation table (these values are the row headings) and which database field contains the values you want to display across the top of the cross-tabulation table (these values are the column headings).

5. Select Continue. The Crosstab Data Options dialog box appears.

6. Specify which database field you want to summarize as well as the type of calculation you want to perform.

7. Select Continue. 1-2-3 for Windows calculates the cross-tabulation table and places it on a new sheet following the current sheet.

To create an aggregate

The **T**ools Data**b**ase Cross**t**ab command creates a new table of cross-tabulated data; the Query **A**ggregate command produces a similar summary in a single column of an existing query table. To create an aggregate, follow these steps:

1. If you have not already created a query table, use **T**ools Data**b**ase **N**ew Query to create a query table.

> **Shortcut**
>
> Click the Query Table SmartIcon.

2 In the query table you created, click the heading of the column for which you want to produce an aggregate analysis.

3 Select **Q**uery **A**ggregate. The Aggregate dialog box appears.

> **Shortcut**
>
> Click the Query Aggregate SmartIcon.

4 Select the analysis to perform.

5 Choose OK. The query table now shows the summary values in the specified column.

Connecting to an External Database

You can use 1-2-3 for Windows' file-translation capabilities or the **T**ools Data**b**ase **C**onnect to External command to access database files created in dBASE, Paradox, SQL Server, Lotus Notes, Informix, Oracle 6 and 7, IBM DB2/2, and Lotus 1-2-3 ODBC.

To connect to an external database

1 Choose either **T**ools Data**b**ase **N**ew Query **E**xternal or **T**ools Data**b**ase **C**onnect to External. The Connect to External dialog box appears.

2 If more than one driver name is shown in the **S**elect a Driver box, highlight the name of the driver you want to use and then select **C**ontinue.

If the selected DataLens driver accepts a password, the Driver Password dialog box appears. If a user ID and password are required on your system, enter the information in the appropriate boxes, and click OK or press Enter. If your system does not require this information, simply click OK or press Enter to continue.

3 The text-box prompt in the Connect to External dialog box changes to **S**elect a Database or Directory. Select the database, and then choose **C**ontinue.

4 Again, the text-box prompt changes—this time to **S**elect a Table. The *table* is the name of the database file you want to use. Select the table, and choose **C**ontinue.

5 The text-box prompt changes to Refer To As. Assigning a range name to the external database table enables you to use Query commands to access the external table.

If the Refer To As text box is blank, the external database's file name is already in use as a 1-2-3 for Windows range name. Specify a different name for the range name you want to assign to the external database file.

6 Choose OK.

If you chose **T**ools Data**b**ase **N**ew Query **E**xternal in step 1, complete the selections in the New Query dialog box, and choose OK again.

After you establish a connection with an external database table, use **T**ools Data**b**ase C**r**eate Table to create an external table; use **T**ools Data**b**ase **S**end Command to send a command to the external database; or use **T**ools Data**b**ase Disc**o**nnect to break the connection between 1-2-3 and the external table. You also can use the **Q**uery commands discussed earlier in this section to manipulate data in external database tables.

Decimal Places

1-2-3 for Windows displays numbers with up to 15 decimal places. By default, negative numbers have a minus sign and decimal values have leading zeros. You can control the number of decimal places displayed with a number by formatting the number. Formatting the number does not actually change the value—it merely displays the value with more or fewer decimal places. For example, the number 2.49503 may be displayed as 2.5, but the entire number is used for calculations. However, if you actually round the value, 1-2-3 uses the rounded value for calculations.

To establish a fixed number of decimal places for cell formats

1. Highlight the cell or range you want to format with a fixed number of decimal places.

2. Choose **S**tyle **N**umber Format. The Number Format dialog box appears.

3. In the **F**ormat list box, select Fixed.

4. Specify the number of decimal places or use the default number, 2, shown in the **D**ecimal Places spin box.

    To change the number of decimal places, type another number between 0 and 15 or use the scroll arrows to change the number.

5. Click OK to close the Number Format dialog box and change the format of the selected range to display the fixed number of decimal places.

> **Note**
>
> The format selector in the status bar displays the format of the current cell. For example, Fixed appears on the format selector when the current cell is formatted with the Fixed format. The number of decimal places for the current cell appears on the decimal selector.

To round a number to a specific number of decimal places

1 Double-click the cell containing the value you want to round.

2 Edit the data in the cell to read @ROUND(data,2). The word *data* represents the existing information in the cell, whether a value or formula. Change the 2 to any number of decimal places you want to use. If the cell contains the formula @D5*H2, for example, you would change it to @ROUND(D5*H2,1) to round to one decimal place.

> **Shortcut**
>
> Click the Comma Format SmartIcon to round a number and display thousand separators and no decimal places.

To remove decimal values from numbers

1 Double-click the cell containing the value for which you want the integer portion.

2 Edit the data in the cell to read @INT(data). The word *data* represents the existing information in the cell, whether a value or formula. If the cell contains the formula @D5*H2, for example, you would change it to @INT(D5*H2).

To remove the integer portion of a number

1 Double-click the cell containing the value for which you want the decimal portion.

2 Edit the data in the cell to read +(data)-@INT(data). The word *data* represents the existing information in the cell, whether a value or formula. If the cell contains the formula @D5*H2, for example, you would change it to +(D5*H2)-@INT(D5*H2).

To set decimal places for all numeric values in the worksheet

1 Choose **S**tyle **W**orksheet Defaults. The Worksheet Defaults dialog box appears.

2 In the F**o**rmat drop-down list box of the Number Format area, choose a number format that uses decimal places, such as Fixed, Scientific, Comma, Currency, or Percent.

3 In the **D**ecimals spin box, specify the number of decimal places you want to use for all numeric values in the worksheet.

4 Choose OK.

> **Tip**
>
> You can use the **R**eset button in the Number Format dialog box to quickly restore the default number format (that is, the format specified in the Worksheet Defaults dialog box) to the selected cell or range.

See also *Number Formatting*.

Deleting Files

When you create and save a file, the file occupies disk space. Eventually, you run out of disk space if you do not occasionally delete old, unneeded files from the disk. Even if you have disk space left, you have more difficulty finding the files you want to open if the disk contains many obsolete files. 1-2-3 for Windows does not provide a command for deleting unneeded files. You must use the Windows File Manager or a DOS command.

Deleting Cells and Ranges

See *Erasing Cells and Ranges*

Deleting Rows, Columns, and Worksheets

When you *erase* cells with **E**dit Cl**e**ar or **E**dit Cu**t**, the cells still exist in the worksheet, but they are empty. In contrast, when you *delete* a worksheet, row, or column, 1-2-3 for Windows removes the entire worksheet, row, or column and moves others to fill the gap created by the deletion. 1-2-3 for Windows also updates addresses, including those in formulas.

To delete a row, column, or worksheet

1 Choose **E**dit **D**elete. The Delete dialog box appears.

2 Choose **C**olumn, **R**ow, or **S**heet, depending on what you want to delete.

3 In the R**a**nge text box, specify the range to be deleted. You can type the address, highlight cells, or preselect cells.

4 Click OK or press Enter to confirm the information in the dialog box and delete the specified area.

Shortcut
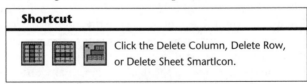 Click the Delete Column, Delete Row, or Delete Sheet SmartIcon.

Another method of deleting is to highlight the rows, columns, or worksheet, then press Ctrl+gray –. Lotus refers to the minus key on the numeric keypad as the gray –.

When you delete a column, 1-2-3 for Windows moves subsequent columns to the left to fill the gap caused by the deletion. When you delete a row or worksheet, 1-2-3 for Windows moves up the remaining rows and worksheets.

If you delete worksheets, rows, or columns that are part of a named range, the range becomes smaller. If you delete the rows and columns of an entire named range, 1-2-3 for Windows deletes the range *and* its name; formulas that refer to that range name result in ERR.

> **Caution**
>
> Usually, deleting rows or columns affects only the current worksheet. If, however, you have grouped together several worksheets with Group mode, when you delete (or add) rows or columns in one worksheet, you delete (or add) the same rows or columns in all the grouped worksheets.

Dialog Editor

The Dialog Editor is a separate program, usually installed when you install 1-2-3 for Windows. This program enables you to create custom dialog boxes for use in 1-2-3 for Windows macro programs that use the DIALOG command.

You can use *custom dialog boxes* to display messages, to prompt the user for input, or to present an entire series of options in a complex application. You can add push buttons, default push buttons, radio buttons, check boxes, edit boxes, list boxes, static text, combo boxes, or group boxes to custom dialog boxes. 1-2-3 stores in the worksheet any response the user makes so that macro programs can examine and use the stored information.

To create a custom dialog box
1. Start the Dialog Editor by clicking the Lotus Dialog Box Editor icon in the Windows Program Manager. The Lotus Dialog Editor window appears.

74 Dialog Editor

> **Shortcut**
>
> Click the Lotus Dialog Editor SmartIcon from within 1-2-3 for Windows.

2 You use the Lotus Dialog Editor window to create and edit custom dialog boxes. There are four drop-down menus.

Use the **F**ile menu commands to create, save, and open dialog-box files and to exit the Dialog Editor. The **E**dit menu commands enable you to copy dialog-box descriptions to and from 1-2-3; cut, copy, and paste dialog-box objects; and change the appearance of dialog-box objects. The **C**ontrol menu enables you to select objects you want to place in a dialog box. The **O**ptions menu offers basic controls to help you use the Dialog Editor itself.

3 To start a new custom dialog box, choose **F**ile **N**ew from the Lotus Dialog Editor window. The New dialog box appears.

> **Shortcut**
>
> Click the Create File SmartIcon.

4 The New dialog box creates a basic dialog box that contains no objects. You later add objects to the empty dialog box.

5 Enter a name in the Dialog Box **N**ame text box. For this example, enter **NEWDIALOG1** in the text box. You use this name in macros to refer to the custom dialog box. If you include more than one custom dialog box in a worksheet application, provide different names for each custom dialog box.

6 If you want the dialog box to display a title, enter the text of the title in the Dialog Box **T**itle text box. If you do not include a title, the title bar does not appear on your custom dialog box.

7 Select Title **B**ar to display just the title; select Title Bar with **S**ystem Menu to include a Control menu in the dialog-box title bar. Select **P**lain to omit both the title bar and Control menu. If you include a Control menu, the user can use the Control menu to close or move the dialog box.

8 Choose OK.

9 Click the mouse anywhere in the Lotus Dialog Editor window to create the basic dialog box in the default size. If necessary, you can change the size of the dialog box by clicking inside the dialog box and then dragging the selection handles to the correct size.

10 Add objects to the dialog box by selecting objects from the **C**ontrol menu or by clicking the appropriate SmartIcon and then clicking the location where you want to add the object. Double-click an object, such as static text, to edit the default text. To resize an object, click the object to select it and drag the selection handles.

11 Choose **F**ile Save **A**s to save the custom dialog box. The Save As dialog box appears. Enter the name of the file in the File **N**ame text box and choose OK.

To copy a custom dialog box to 1-2-3

The only way to add a custom dialog box to 1-2-3 is to copy the dialog box from the Dialog Editor to the Clipboard and then paste it into 1-2-3. You do not paste the actual dialog box into 1-2-3, however. Instead, you paste a *dialog-description table* (information used by 1-2-3 to duplicate the dialog box).

To copy the dialog box to 1-2-3, follow these steps (starting in the Dialog Editor):

1 Choose **F**ile **O**pen. The Open dialog box appears. Enter the file name in the File **N**ame text box and choose OK.

2 Make certain that none of the individual dialog-box objects are selected.

3 Select **E**dit **C**opy.

> **Shortcut**
>
> Click the Copy SmartIcon.

4 Use Ctrl+Esc or Alt+Tab to return to 1-2-3 for Windows. If you have not already started 1-2-3 for Windows, return to the Program Manager and start 1-2-3 for Windows.

5 Select an empty location in the worksheet for the dialog-description table. You may want to create a separate worksheet for dialog-description tables to keep from overwriting existing data.

6 Select **E**dit **P**aste. The dialog-description table appears in the worksheet.

> **Shortcut**
>
> Click the Paste SmartIcon.

To test the dialog box

The next step is to test the dialog box to make certain that it works correctly. For this step, you use the DIALOG macro command.

First, create a range name for the dialog-description table. You can select **R**ange **N**ame **U**se Labels and choose To The Left from the **F**or Cells list to apply the name, NEWDIALOG1, to the upper left corner of the dialog-description table.

Then create a macro that contains the following single command:

```
{DIALOG NEWDIALOG1}
```

Name this macro \d and then run the macro. 1-2-3 displays the custom dialog box. (For more information on creating and naming this macro, see *Macros*.)

To test the dialog box, add text to the edit boxes and then choose OK or Cancel to close the dialog box and end the macro. When the macro ends, the dialog box is cleared from the screen. If the dialog box does not display when you run the macro, make certain that the macro refers to the correct range (the dialog-description table). In particular, make certain that the name of the dialog box is assigned to the DIALOG label in the dialog-description table.

Drawing

In addition to adding charts to the worksheet, you can enhance your presentation of data with drawn objects. *Drawn objects* are graphic elements such as text blocks, arrows, and circles. The **T**ools **D**raw commands and several SmartIcons enable you to access and draw these elements.

Drawing Objects

The procedures for creating the most common types of objects are described in the following sections. Other objects are created in a similar manner.

78 Drawing

To create a text block

1 Choose **T**ools **D**raw **T**ext.

> **Shortcut**
>
> Click the Text Block SmartIcon.

You are prompted to click and drag to draw a text block. A *text block* is the container for your descriptive text.

2 To draw the text block, place the mouse pointer on the chart or worksheet in which you want the text to go, and then click and drag to create a box the approximate height and width of the text block you are entering.

3 After drawing the box, type the text in the block. To enter multiple lines of text, either let the text word wrap or press Enter after each line.

To edit the text later, double-click the text block. A cursor appears at the beginning of the text. Use the mouse or arrow keys to position the cursor, and make your corrections.

See also *Text Blocks*.

To add lines and arrows

To add lines and arrows to emphasize specific areas in a chart or worksheet, follow these steps:

1 Choose **T**ools **D**raw **L**ine or **T**ools **D**raw **A**rrow.

> **Shortcut**
>
>   Click the Draw Line or the Draw Arrow SmartIcon.

After you select the drawing tool, the mouse pointer changes to a cross and 1-2-3 prompts you to click and drag to draw the line or arrow.

Drawing **79**

2 Place the cross at the location where you want the line or arrow to begin, and then click and drag to where you want the line or arrow to end.

3 After you reach the end of the line, simply release the mouse button. If you are creating an arrow, an arrowhead appears at the point where you release the mouse button.

1-2-3 for Windows displays a line or arrow on the chart or worksheet, with handles to indicate that the line or arrow is selected. While selected, the line or arrow can be moved or changed.

To draw a rectangle or ellipse

1 Choose **T**ools **D**raw **R**ectangle or **T**ools **D**raw **E**llipse.

Shortcut	
▢ ⬭	Click the Draw Rectangle or Draw Ellipse SmartIcon.

2 Position the pointer where you want the rectangle or ellipse to begin and drag the mouse until the rectangle or ellipse is the desired size and shape.

To create a square or circle, hold the Shift key as you drag the mouse.

3 Release the mouse button.

> **Tip**
>
> If you hold down the Shift key as you draw an ellipse or rectangle, 1-2-3 creates a perfect circle or square. If you press Shift while drawing an arc, 1-2-3 creates a perfect semicircle. Press Shift while drawing a line or arrow and you get a perfectly horizontal, vertical, or 45-degree diagonal line.

Arranging Objects

After you have drawn objects on the sheet, you can move them around to make them work together. Because 1-2-3's drawing capabilities are object-oriented, each object appears on an invisible "layer" above the worksheet. You may want to change how the objects overlap each other. You also can combine objects into groups; a group behaves as a single object.

To move an object around the page

1. Click the object and hold down the mouse button.

2. Drag the object to the new location. The mouse pointer looks like a hand while you are dragging. Release the mouse button when you finish.

If you have to move an object a large distance within a worksheet or between two sheets, first choose **E**dit Cu**t** or press Ctrl+X to remove the object from its original location. Move to the new location, and then choose **E**dit **P**aste or press Ctrl+V to place the object into the new position.

Shortcut

  You also can move an object by selecting the object, clicking the Cut SmartIcon, moving to the new location, and then pressing Enter or clicking the Paste SmartIcon.

To bring an object to the front or back of others

If you draw an ellipse on top of a text block, the text is hidden, because all objects are stacked on top of one another in the order you create them. Thus an ellipse can be on top of a text block that is on top of a chart.

1. Click the object once to select it.

2. From the **E**dit **A**rrange menu, choose **B**ring to Front or **S**end to Back, depending on which object is selected.

These commands send an object all the way to the back or bring it all the way to the front; you cannot move an object forward or backward by only one layer.

Shortcut
Click the Move Object to Front or the Move Object to Back SmartIcon.

To combine objects into a group

1 Click the first object in the group.

2 Hold down the Shift key and click all other objects in the group. All the objects should remain selected.

3 From the **E**dit **A**rrange menu, choose **G**roup. The grouped object can be copied or moved as a single group.

4 To return a grouped object to its original, independent elements, highlight the group, then choose **E**dit **A**rrange Un**g**roup.

To copy objects

1 Click the object to select it.

2 Choose **E**dit **C**opy to copy the object.

Shortcut
Press Ctrl+C,
or
Click the Copy SmartIcon.

3 Click the mouse pointer at the desired location.

4 Choose **E**dit **P**aste or press Ctrl+V to place a copy of the object in the new position.

> **Shortcut**
>
> Press Enter,
>
> or
>
> Click the Paste SmartIcon.

To copy an object with drag-and-drop

1 Click the object and hold down the mouse button.

2 Hold the Ctrl key down as you drag the object to its new location. When you reach the destination, release the mouse and the Ctrl key.

1-2-3 for Windows copies the object to the new location without changing the original.

To drag-and-drop to another sheet

You may want to copy the object to a distant area in the worksheet, or to a separate sheet in the worksheet. You can still use drag-and-drop if you first window the two areas.

1 Choose **V**iew **S**plit. The sheet splits into two windows.

2 In one of the windows, scroll to display the object to be moved.

3 In the other window, click a sheet tab or the New Sheet button if the object is to be copied to another sheet. Scroll to the area of the sheet where the object will be copied.

4 Click the object and hold down the mouse button.

5 Hold down the Ctrl key as you drag the object to its new location in the other window. The mouse pointer looks like a hand while you are dragging. When you reach the destination, release the mouse and the Ctrl key.

To drag-and-drop to another file

1 Open the source file and the file to which you want to copy the object, the destination file.

2 Choose **W**indow **T**ile to display the files side by side. Scroll each window to make the source and destination areas visible.

3 Click the object and hold down the mouse button.

4 Drag the object to its new location in the other window. The mouse pointer looks like a hand while you are dragging. When you reach the destination, release the mouse button.

It is not necessary to hold down the Ctrl key to drag-and-drop to another file. The object remains in the original file.

To delete an object

1 Click the object to select it. You may select several objects to delete by holding down the Shift key while selecting other objects.

2 Choose **E**dit Cu**t** or press Ctrl+X.

Shortcut
Press the Del key
or
Click the Cut SmartIcon.

Editing Data

After you enter data in a cell, you may want to change the data. You can change an existing entry in either of two ways. You can replace the contents of a cell by typing a new entry, or you can change part of a cell's contents by editing the cell.

To replace the contents of a cell, move the cell pointer to the cell you want to change, type the new data, and press Enter.

To edit a cell's contents, you must be in Edit mode. You can enter Edit mode in three ways. You can move the mouse pointer to the contents box; the shape of the pointer changes from an arrow to an I-beam. Move the I-beam to the area you want to change and then click the mouse button. You also can move the cell pointer to the cell and press F2 (Edit) to enter Edit mode. Finally, you can double-click the cell.

You can edit data, including formulas, either in the contents box or directly in the cell. The in-cell editing capability enables you to turn off the edit line of the control panel (using **V**iew Set View **P**references) to display more rows in the worksheet.

When 1-2-3 for Windows is in Edit mode, a cursor flashes in the cell, or if you click the contents box, the cursor flashes in the contents box. You use the editing keys to move the cursor. Edit the cell contents, then press Enter or click the green check-mark icon to complete the edit.

If you press Esc or click the red X icon while 1-2-3 for Windows is in Edit mode, you clear the cell and the contents box and return the cell to its earlier state. If you press Enter while the edit area is blank, you do not erase the cell's contents, and you return to Ready mode.

Entering Data

To enter data into a worksheet, move the cell pointer to the appropriate cell, type the entry, and press Enter. As you type, the entry appears in the contents box and in the cell. If you enter data into a cell that already contains information, the new data replaces the old.

Another way to enter information into a cell is to double-click the cell. Double-clicking places the *cursor* (the flashing bar) in the cell, and you can begin typing.

If you plan to enter data into more than one cell, you can enter data and move the cell pointer with one keystroke; press a direction key (for example, Tab, PgDn, or an arrow key) after typing the entry.

You can create two kinds of cell entries: label and value. A *label* is a text entry, and a *value* is a number or a formula. 1-2-3 for Windows determines the kind of cell entry from the first character you enter.

1-2-3 considers an entry to be a value (a number or a formula) if the entry begins with one of the following characters:

    0 1 2 3 4 5 6 7 8 9 + - (@ # . $

If the entry begins with any other character, 1-2-3 considers the entry to be a label. When you type the first character, the mode indicator changes from Ready to Value or Label.

To enter labels

Labels make the numbers and formulas in worksheets understandable. You can use labels for titles, row and column headings, and descriptive text that appears in your worksheets. A label can be a string of up to 512 characters.

When you enter a label, 1-2-3 for Windows adds a *label prefix* to the cell entry. The label prefix is visible in both the worksheet and the contents box. 1-2-3 uses the label prefix to identify the entry as a label and to determine how to display and print the entry. By default, the program uses an apostrophe (') for a left-aligned label. To use a different label prefix, type one of the following prefixes as the first character of the label:

Prefix	Description
'	Left-aligned (the default)
"	Right-aligned
^	Centered
\	Repeating

If you want a label prefix character to appear as the first character of a label, you first must type a label prefix and then type another label prefix as the first character of the label. If you type **\015** in a cell, for example, the program displays 015015015015015015 as a repeating label. You first must type a label prefix—here, an apostrophe (')—and then type **\015**.

You also must type a label prefix if the first character of the label is a numeric character. If you do not type a prefix, 1-2-3 for Windows switches to Value mode when you type the numeric character because the program expects a valid number or formula to follow. If the label contains numbers and is a valid formula—for example, the telephone number (317-555-6100)—1-2-3 evaluates the entry as a formula.

If a typed label such as an address (338 Main Street) results in an invalid formula, 1-2-3 for Windows assumes the entry is a label and supplies the prefix.

If a label is longer than a cell's width, 1-2-3 displays the label across all blank cells to the right of the cell. The data is not actually filling all these cells but is spilling across them. A long text entry may spill across several blank cells.

If the cells to the right of the label cell are not blank, 1-2-3 for Windows cuts off the display of the entry at the cell border. The program still stores the complete entry in the contents box, however, and displays the full entry when the cell is highlighted.

To display the entire label in the worksheet, you can insert blank columns to the right of the cell containing the long label, or you can widen the column. Widening the column is easy when you use the mouse; simply click the column border to the right of the column letter and drag the border to the desired width. Or, to automatically adjust the column width to the widest entry, double-click the right border of the column heading.

> **Shortcut**
>
> Click the column heading to highlight the column, and then click the Size Columns SmartIcon.

To enter values
To enter a valid number in a worksheet, you can type any of the 10 digits (0 through 9) and certain other characters, such as pluses, minuses, and percent signs.

1-2-3 for Windows stores only 18 digits of any number. If you enter a number with more than 18 digits, 1-2-3 rounds the number after the 18th digit. The program stores the complete number (up to 18 digits) but displays only what fits in the cell.

If the number is too long to display in the cell, 1-2-3 for Windows tries to display as much of the number as possible. If the cell uses the default General format and the integer part of the number fits into the cell, 1-2-3 rounds the decimal characters that don't fit. If the integer part of the number doesn't fit in the cell, the program displays the number in *scientific (exponential) notation*. If the cell uses a format other than General or the cell width is too narrow to display in scientific notation and the number cannot fit into the cell, 1-2-3 for Windows displays asterisks.

You also can type a number in scientific notation. 1-2-3 stores a number in scientific notation only if it contains more than 20 digits. If you enter a number with more than 18 digits, 1-2-3 rounds the number to end with one or more zeros.

The appearance of a number in the worksheet depends on the cell's format, font, and column width. When you use the default font (12-point Arial MT) and the default column width (9), 1-2-3 displays the number 1234567890 as `1.2E+09`. If you use a column width of 11, however, 1-2-3 displays the number as entered.

Erasing Cells and Ranges

You can clear part or all of the worksheet in several ways. Any data that you clear is removed from memory, but these changes don't affect the file on disk until you save the current version of the file to disk. You can use either of two commands to erase a cell or range: **E**dit Cl**e**ar or **E**dit Cu**t**.

The **E**dit Cl**e**ar command lets you erase all data (label, value, formula, or function), attributes, and formats from a cell or range. Alternatively, you can erase only the styles or content of a cell. Choose the desired option from the Clear dialog box that appears when you use the **E**dit Cl**e**ar command.

Shortcut

Press Del (Delete).

or

 Click the Delete SmartIcon.

The **E**dit Cu**t** command is designed to be followed with the **E**dit **P**aste command. The **E**dit Cu**t** command removes the selected range from the worksheet (including all data, attributes, and format) and places the range on the Windows

Erasing Cells and Ranges

Clipboard, a holding area in memory. With the **E**dit **P**aste command, you can choose to have this information pasted to other locations from the Clipboard. You can use **E**dit **P**aste repeatedly to paste the same data in various locations. If you want to remove data so that it can be pasted elsewhere, use **E**dit **Cu**t, not **E**dit **Cl**ear.

Shortcut

Press Shift+Del to cut, and press Shift+Ins to paste.

or

   Click the Cut and Paste SmartIcons.

To use drag-and-clear to delete data

You can also clear data from a range by using the mouse to drag-and-clear. Drag-and-clear does not clear protected cells, 3D ranges, collections, drawn objects, or query tables.

1 Highlight the range you want to clear.

Drag-and-clear will not clear the top left cell of the range. If the cells adjacent to the top or left edge of the range are clear, you may highlight these cells with the range in order to clear all of the data.

2 Position the mouse pointer at the lower right corner of the range, until the pointer changes to an arrow with small horizontal and vertical double arrowheads.

3 Click the left mouse button and drag to the top left cell of the range.

4 Release the mouse button. The data in the range is erased.

Exiting 1-2-3 for Windows

Microsoft Windows applications can open multiple document windows. 1-2-3 for Windows enables you to close individual worksheet windows or to exit 1-2-3 entirely, closing all open windows.

To exit 1-2-3 for Windows

1 Choose File Exit. If you have saved changes in active worksheet files, 1-2-3 closes. If you have not saved changes to active files, a confirmation box appears.

> **Shortcut**
>
> Press Alt+F4.
>
> or
>
> Click the End 1-2-3 Session SmartIcon.

2 If the Exit confirmation box appears, choose Yes or press Enter to save the current worksheet file before exiting; choose No to exit without saving the file; choose Cancel to cancel the Exit command and return to 1-2-3 for Windows. If you have multiple Worksheet windows open, select Save All to save all files before exiting.

To quit 1-2-3 for Windows and return to the Program Manager, you also can double-click the 1-2-3 Control menu box. If the Exit confirmation box appears, make your selection as outlined in step 2.

Filling Ranges

The Range Fill and Range Fill By Example commands enable you to fill ranges with data, such as a Record Number field in a database, a series of dates or titles, and a series of interest-rate entries. You can fill ranges with a series of numbers (which can be in the form of numbers, formulas, or functions), dates, or times that increase or decrease by a specified increment or decrement.

Filling Ranges **91**

1-2-3 for Windows fills the range from top to bottom and left to right. The first cell is filled with the start value, and each subsequent cell is filled with the value in the preceding cell plus the increment. Filling stops when 1-2-3 for Windows reaches the stop value or the end of the fill range, whichever happens first.

To fill a range

1 Highlight the range you want to fill with data and choose **R**ange **F**ill. The Fill dialog box appears.

> **Shortcut**
>
> Click the Fill Range SmartIcon.

2 Enter the starting number of the series in the **S**tart text box.

3 Enter the incremental value to be added in the **I**ncrement text box.

4 Enter the ending value in the St**o**p text box.

5 Choose OK.

You also can use formulas and functions for the start, step (incremental), and stop values. If you want to fill a range of cells with incrementing dates after the range is set, you can use the @DATE function to set the start value. You also can use a cell formula, such as +E4, for the incremental value.

To fill a range with dates or times

Range **F**ill also enables you to fill a worksheet range with a sequence of dates or times without using values, formulas, or functions. You specify the starting and stopping values, the increment between values, and the interval. Select from the following options in the Interval box to specify the interval: **L**inear, **Y**ear, **Q**uarter, **M**onth, **W**eek, **D**ay, **H**our, Mi**n**ute, and Se**c**ond. The **L**inear option adds the number specified by **I**ncrement to the preceding value. All other interval options add the number of date or time intervals specified by **I**ncrement to the preceding value.

When you use one of the time intervals to fill a range, 1-2-3 for Windows automatically formats the range with an appropriate date or time format. In addition, the program automatically supplies the current date as a default starting value (which you can change).

To create a fill sequence

1-2-3 for Windows offers an even easier method of filling ranges with values: the **R**ange Fill By **E**xample command can determine the correct fill sequence for many different types of data. You can use dates, times, month or day names, and incrementing labels (such as Qtr 1) as starting values. Follow these steps:

1 Enter one or more values in the worksheet to show 1-2-3 for Windows how to fill the range. Some examples (shown with the resulting sequences) include the following:

Data You Enter	Resulting Sequence
1994	1995, 1996, 1997...
Jan	Feb, Mar, Apr...
2, 4	6, 8, 10, 12...
Qtr 1	Qtr 2, Qtr 3, Qtr 4...

2 Highlight the range you want to fill and choose **R**ange Fill By **E**xample.

Shortcut

 Click the Fill Range by Example SmartIcon.

1-2-3 for Windows then examines the values in the worksheet to determine the correct pattern and uses that pattern to fill the selected range. You do not need to specify a **S**tart, **I**ncrement, St**o**p, or Interval.

To create a custom fill sequence

If you often enter the same set of labels in your worksheets, you may want to create your own custom fill sequences for use with **R**ange Fill By **E**xample. For example, you can create a custom fill sequence that enters region names, store locations, and sales representatives' names.

Custom fill sequences are stored in a text file, FILLS.INI, which usually is located in the \123R5W\PROGRAMS directory. You can edit this file with the Windows Notepad, the DOS Edit command, or any other text editor that does not add special codes. (Most word processing programs add formatting information as special codes.)

Custom fill sequences are stored as numbered sets in FILLS.INI. Each custom fill sequence must follow certain rules:

- The first line of each set must consist of [SET #] (where # is the set number).

- You must list the items in order in lines that begin with ITEM#= (where # is the item number).

- To make 1-2-3 for Windows enter the data in the same combination of uppercase and lowercase letters that appear in the list, type **CASE=EXACT** on a separate line anywhere in the list. Otherwise, 1-2-3 for Windows determines case based on the label in the first cell of the range that you want to fill.

When you make all your additions or corrections, save the file. To add a special list of location names, for example, you could add the following text to FILLS.INI:

> [SET 4]
> CASE=EXACT
> ITEM1=Chicago
> ITEM2=Denver
>
> ITEM3=Los Angeles
> ITEM4=New York
> ITEM5=Orlando

Then, if you enter **Chicago** in a cell of the worksheet, select a range of five cells (with Chicago in the first cell), and choose **R**ange Fill by **E**xample, the remaining four items appear in the specified range.

To use drag-and-fill to enter a sequence

You can also use the mouse to quickly fill a range with a sequence of data, including custom fill sequences. For example, you can enter **Mercury** in a cell and then drag to fill a range with Venus, Earth, Mars, Jupiter, and so forth.

1 Select the cell or range representing the sequence you want to continue. For example, enter **JAN** in cell A1.

2 Position the mouse pointer at the lower right corner of the range, until the pointer changes to an arrow with small horizontal and vertical double arrows.

3 Click the left mouse button and drag down or to the right to select the range you want to fill. For example, drag to the right to select the range A1..L1.

4 Release the mouse button. The range fills with the abbreviated names of the months, JAN to DEC.

Finding and Replacing Data

Edit **F**ind & Replace finds and/or replaces characters in a range of labels and formulas; this command works much like the search-and-replace feature in many word processing programs.

To find and replace data

1 Highlight the range to search. (This step is optional; you can specify the range from the Find & Replace dialog box.)

2 Choose **E**dit **F**ind & Replace. The Find & Replace dialog box appears.

> **Shortcut**
>
> Click the Find SmartIcon.

3 Enter the search string into the **S**earch For text box.

4 Specify the type of search: **L**abels, **F**ormulas, or **B**oth.

5 Specify the action: **F**ind or Replace **W**ith.

6 Enter the replacement string in the Replace **W**ith text box.

7 Choose OK. The Replace dialog box appears.

8 In the Replace dialog box, choose **R**eplace, Replace **A**ll, Find **N**ext, or Close.

You may want to choose **R**eplace for the first occurrence and then make sure that the change is made correctly. If it is correct, choose Replace **A**ll to replace the other occurrences. If the replacement isn't correct, close the dialog box and try again. If you want to replace only certain occurrences, choose Find **N**ext and then choose **R**eplace for each appropriate occurrence.

If you choose Find **N**ext instead of Replace **A**ll as the search mode, the cell pointer moves to the first cell in the range. Choose Find **N**ext to find the next occurrence, or choose Close or press Esc to cancel the search and return to Ready mode. If there are no more matching strings, 1-2-3 for Windows displays an error message and stops searching. At the end of a replace operation, the cell pointer remains at the last cell replaced.

You also can use **E**dit **F**ind & Replace to modify formulas. If you have many formulas that round to two decimal places, such as @ROUND(A1*B1,2), you can change the formulas to round to four decimal places with a search string of **,2**) and a replace string of **,4**).

Be extremely careful when you replace numbers in formulas. If you try to replace 2 with 4, the formula @ROUND(A2*B2,2) becomes @ROUND(A4*B4,4).

An incorrect search-and-replace operation can harm a file. You should first save the file before performing **E**dit **F**ind & Replace, even though you can undo an incorrect search.

Fonts and Attributes

A *typeface* is a particular style of type, such as Arial MT or Times New Roman PS. Typefaces can have different *attributes*, such as weight (regular, bold, italic) and underline. Most typefaces are available in a number of point sizes. The *point size* describes the height of the characters (there are 72 points in an inch). The most commonly used point sizes for "standard" print are 10 point and 12 point. Titles and headings are often set in 14-point or 18-point type.

A typeface of a given point size with a given set of attributes is called a *font*. In practice, many people use the terms *typeface* and *font* interchangeably, although they have different meanings. In 1-2-3 for Windows, a *font* is a typeface of a given size.

To change the typeface, point size, and attributes for a cell or range, use one of the following methods:

- Choose **S**tyle **F**ont & Attributes to open the Font & Attributes dialog box. Change the settings as desired. If you select **U**nderline, specify an underline style with the drop-down box. You can also change the color of the font with the **C**olor drop-down box. The Sample box shows how the font and other attributes you select will look in the worksheet. Select OK to close the dialog box and apply the font to the selected cell or range.

Shortcut
Click the Font & Attributes SmartIcon.

Fonts and Attributes **97**

- Select the cell or range to change and click the font selector or point-size selector in the status bar to reveal a pop-up list of choices. Select the font and point size from the list with the mouse or arrow keys.

- To apply bold, italic, or underline to a selected cell or range, use the following SmartIcons. You can apply several attributes by clicking on more than one of these formatting SmartIcons.

> **Shortcut**
>
> 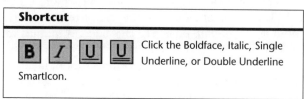 Click the Boldface, Italic, Single Underline, or Double Underline SmartIcon.

If necessary, 1-2-3 for Windows enlarges the row height to fit the selected fonts. However, 1-2-3 for Windows does not adjust column widths automatically. After you change a font, numeric data may no longer fit in the columns and may display as asterisks. Change the column widths as needed to correctly display the data.

> **Tip**
>
> Use the Normal Format SmartIcon to remove bold face, italic, and underlining all at once from selected cells. (You can also use the Attribute SmartIcons to remove an attribute.)

Formatting

See *Number Formatting* or *Styling Data*

Formulas

The real power of 1-2-3 for Windows comes from the program's capability to calculate formulas. Formulas make 1-2-3 an electronic worksheet, not just a computerized way to assemble data. You enter the numbers and formulas into the worksheet, and 1-2-3 for Windows calculates the results of all the formulas.

You can enter formulas that perform calculations on numbers, labels, and other cells in the worksheet. Like a label, a formula can contain up to 512 characters. A formula can include numbers, text, operators, cell and range addresses, range names, and functions. A formula cannot include spaces except within a range name or text string. The contents box shows the formula, and the worksheet shows the result of the calculation. This result changes when you change any number in the referenced cells.

Formulas can operate on numbers in cells. The formula 8+26 uses 1-2-3 for Windows as a calculator. A more useful formula involves cell references in the calculation. For example, you can use the following simple formula to add the values in two cells on the same worksheet:

    +A1+B1

This formula indicates that the value stored in cell A1 will be added to the value stored in B1. 1-2-3 recalculates the formula if you enter new data. For example, if A1 originally contains the value 4 and if B1 contains the value 3, the formula results in the value 7. If you change the value in A1 to 5, 1-2-3 recalculates the formula to 8.

You use *operators* in numeric, string, and logical formulas to specify the calculations to be performed, and in what order. The following table lists the operators in the order in which 1-2-3 for Windows uses them.

Operator	Operation	Precedence
^	Exponentiation	1
-, +	Negative, positive value	2
*, /	Multiplication, division	3
+, -	Addition, subtraction	4
=, <>	Equal to, not equal to	5
<, >	Less than, greater than	5
<=	Less than or equal to	5
>=	Greater than or equal to	5
#NOT#	Logical NOT	6
#AND#	Logical AND	7
#OR#	Logical OR	7
&	String formula	7

The power of 1-2-3 for Windows formulas, however, is best illustrated by the program's capability to link data across worksheets and across worksheet files. By referencing cells in other worksheets and worksheet files, formulas can calculate results from many worksheet applications. To create a formula that links data across worksheets, you first specify the worksheet in which the data is located (indicated by a letter or letters, A through IV, or by a defined worksheet name), followed by a colon (:), and finally the cell address. The following example shows a formula that links data across three worksheets (A, B, and D):

+A:B3+B:C6+D:B4

If the formula links data across worksheet files, you include the file name, surrounded by double-angle brackets. Note the following example:

+A:C6+<<SALES1.WK4>>A:C5

Because formulas do not depend on a specific value in a cell, you can change a value in a cell and see what happens when your formulas are recalculated. This "what-if" capability makes 1-2-3 for Windows an incredibly powerful tool for many types of analysis.

Freezing Titles

Most worksheets are much larger than can be displayed on-screen at one time. As you move the cell pointer, you scroll the display. New data appears at one edge of the display as the data at the other edge scrolls out of sight.

To prevent titles from scrolling off the screen

1. Move the cell pointer to the row and/or column that marks the top-left cell of the "working area" of the sheet. For example, if the titles are in row 1 and column A, select cell B2.

   Everything above and/or to the left of the cell pointer will be frozen.

2. Choose **V**iew Freeze **T**itles. The Freeze Titles dialog box appears.

3. To lock the top rows of the worksheet, select the **R**ows option button. To lock the leftmost columns, select **C**olumns. To lock both rows and columns, select **B**oth.

4. Choose OK.

If you press Home when titles are locked, the cell pointer moves to the position below and to the right of the titles rather than to cell A1.

To unfreeze the titles
    Choose **V**iew Clear **T**itles.

Frequency Distributions

A *frequency distribution* describes the relationship between a set of classes and the frequency of occurrence of members of each class.

Data must be numeric and arranged in a column, row, or rectangular range located in one or more worksheet files, either open or on disk. This is called the *value range*.

The **R**ange **A**nalyze **D**istribution command counts the number of values in the values range that fall within intervals specified in the *bin range*. You cannot include labels or blank cells in the bin range.

To create a frequency distribution
1. Move the cell pointer to a worksheet portion that has two adjacent blank columns. In the left column, enter the highest value for each entry in the bin range. Enter these bin values in ascending order.

2. Choose **R**ange **A**nalyze **D**istribution.

3. Specify the values range, which contains the data being analyzed, in the R**a**nge of Values text box.

4. Specify the bin range containing the intervals in the **B**in Range text box.

5. Choose OK.

The frequency column extends one row beyond the bin range to represent the number of values that exceeds the largest value in the bin range.

Functions

1-2-3 for Windows provides more than 220 built-in formulas, called *functions* (or *@functions*), that enable you to create complex formulas for a wide range of applications, including business, scientific, and engineering. Instead of entering complicated formulas containing many operators and parentheses, you can use functions as a shortcut to creating such formulas.

All functions in 1-2-3 for Windows begin with the @ sign followed by the name of the function, such as @SUM, @RAND, and @ROUND. Many functions require you to enter an *argument*—the specifications the function needs to calculate the formula—after the function name. To add the values contained in range A2 through H2, for example, you can enter **@SUM(A2..H2)**. You also can use range names to specify arguments. If range A2 through H2 is named SALES, for example, you can enter **@SUM(SALES)**.

This section describes the three methods from which you can choose to enter 1-2-3 for Windows functions, followed by a table of the ten function categories.

Entering Functions

To enter a function, you must type it, using the correct syntax, and then press Enter. The result of the formula appears in the cell. You can enter a function into a worksheet cell in any of three ways.

To enter a function directly into the worksheet cell

1 Type the entire function, including arguments, into the cell or contents box using the keyboard.

2 Press Enter. 1-2-3 for Windows displays the results of the function in the cell.

To select a function from the @Function list

1 Type the @ symbol in the cell or contents box.

2 Press F3 (Name) to display the @Function List dialog box, as shown in the following figure.

3 In the Category drop-down list, select a category to narrow down the list of functions. The default category is All @functions.

4 In the @Functions list box, all the functions in the category you selected are listed in alphabetical order. You can select the function you want by scrolling through the list. Or you can move quickly to a function in the list by typing its first letter.

Click the function name to highlight it. A description of the highlighted function is displayed at the bottom of the dialog box.

5 Click OK or press Enter; the function is placed in the current cell. If an argument is required, the argument descriptions are listed in parentheses.

6 Replace the highlighted argument name by typing the required argument, which may be text, a value, a location, or a condition.

In the function syntax lines, optional arguments for functions are enclosed in brackets ([]). You do *not* type these brackets if entering optional arguments.

104 Functions

7 Double-click to highlight each argument name and type the required data.

8 Press Enter to complete the function. 1-2-3 for Windows displays the results of the function in the cell.

To use the @function selector

1 Click the @function selector, the second icon in the edit line (just below the 1-2-3 for Windows menu bar). A drop-down list appears.

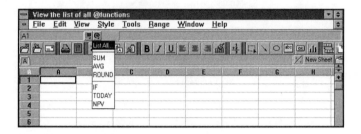

This list includes at least two sections separated by a solid line. The top selection, labeled List All, accesses the @Function List dialog box, which lists all the functions. (Follow steps 4 through 8 in the preceding section to use this dialog box.) The remaining items in the list are commonly used functions.

2 To use a function in this list, click the function, or highlight it and press Enter.

> **Note**
>
> If ERR appears in the cell after you press Enter to complete the function, you have made an error entering the function or its arguments. Perhaps you did not replace each argument with the correct specifications. You can edit the function by double-clicking the cell, or by selecting the cell and editing the function in the contents box.

To quickly sum a range

1 Select a cell next to the range you want to sum.

2 Click the Sum SmartIcon.

The @SUM function is entered for the range and appears in the contents box. The result appears in the cell.

Using Functions

The 1-2-3 for Windows functions are grouped into categories that reflect the purpose of the function, as shown in the following table.

Category	Description
Calendar	Converts dates and times to serial numbers. You then can use the serial numbers in date and time arithmetic—valuable aids if dates and times affect worksheet calculations and logic.
Database	Performs statistical calculations and queries on a 1-2-3 for Windows database or an external database.
Engineering	Performs engineering calculations and advanced mathematical formulas.
Financial	Performs calculations for discounted cash flow, depreciation, bonds, and compound interest. The Financial functions are broken into five major categories: Annuities, Bonds, Capital-Budgeting Tools, Depreciation, and Single-Sum Compounding.
Information	Returns information about cell ranges, the operating system, the Version Manager, and Solver. The Information functions are broken into three major categories: Cell and Range Information, System and Session Information, and Error-Checking.
Logical	Evaluates Boolean expressions, which are true (returning a value of 1) or false (returning a value of 0). Except for @IF, all the Logical functions result in 1 or 0.

(continues)

Category	Description
Lookup	Returns the contents of a cell. With Lookup functions, you use specified keys to locate values in tables or lists.
Mathematical	Performs a variety of standard arithmetic operations. The Mathematical functions are broken into five major categories: Conversion, General, Hyperbolic, Rounding, and Trigonometric.
Statistical	Performs all standard statistical calculations on your worksheet data. The Statistical functions are broken into five major categories: Forecasting, General, Probability, Ranking, and Significance Tests.
Text	Provides information on text in cells and helps you manipulate text.

After you enter a function, you may want to copy the function to other cells. For information on copying a formula (which may contain functions) to another cell, see *Copying Data*.

For a detailed explanation of each function available, refer to Que's *Using 1-2-3 Release 5 for Windows*, Special Edition.

Graphics

The term *graphics* can refer to more than one kind of object in 1-2-3 for Windows. Graphs that you create from worksheet data are called *charts*. You can also import pictures or drawings stored in various formats in an external file. These pictures are often called *clip art*. 1-2-3 for Windows enables you to create your own graphic objects using drawing tools. Refer to the sections describing these particular graphics.

See *Charts* or *Clip Art* or *Drawing*.

Grid Lines

Grid lines appear on the 1-2-3 for Windows screen, but are not printed by default. You can change the appearance of the worksheet on-screen by removing the grid lines, or by changing the color of the grid lines. Likewise, you can also choose to print with or without grid lines.

To turn off grid lines

1. Choose **V**iew Set View **P**references. The Set View Preferences dialog box appears.

2. In the Show in Current File area, select the **G**rid lines check box to remove the x.

3. Choose **M**ake Default if you want all new worksheets that do not use a SmartMaster to use these settings as the default.

4. Choose OK. The grid lines disappear.

To change the color of grid lines

1. Choose **V**iew Set View **P**references. The Set View Preferences dialog box appears.

2. In the Show in Current File area, be sure the **G**rid lines check box is selected, making the color drop-down list available.

3. Choose a color from the drop-down list.

4. Choose **M**ake Default if you want all new worksheets that do not use a SmartMaster to use these settings as the default.

5. Choose OK. The grid lines are the color you selected.

To print the grid lines

1 Choose **F**ile Pa**g**e Setup. The Page Setup dialog box appears.

2 In the Show area, select the **G**rid lines check box.

3 In the Default Settings area, choose **U**pdate to make the current settings the default.

4 Choose OK.

Grouping Worksheets

1-2-3 for Windows enables you to group together all the worksheets in a worksheet file. With grouped worksheets, the changes you make to one worksheet affect all of the other worksheets in the file. You cannot group just selected worksheets; using Group mode means that all of the worksheets in a file are grouped.

When you select a cell or range in one worksheet in a group, the same area is selected (even though it is not highlighted or outlined) in each worksheet in that group. When you format a cell or range in one worksheet, the corresponding area is formatted in each of the other worksheets. Scrolling and moving the cell pointer are also synchronized within the group; therefore, you always see the same part of each worksheet.

To group worksheets

1 Choose **S**tyle **W**orksheet Defaults. The Worksheet Defaults dialog box appears.

2 Select the **G**roup Mode check box.

3 Choose OK. The Group indicator appears in the status bar at the bottom of the screen.

If 1-2-3 for Windows is in Group mode and you use commands that prompt you for a cell address, 1-2-3 for Windows does not need the address of the three-dimensional selection that spans the group—just the range in one of the worksheets. When you complete the command, the effect takes place in all worksheets in the group even if you only refer to cell(s) in one worksheet.

If you want to add one or more worksheets to an existing group, add the new worksheet(s) with the **E**dit **I**nsert **S**heet command or the New Sheet button; the formatting and attributes of the active worksheet are automatically created at the same time. 1-2-3 for Windows does not copy any data, only cell attributes. If Group mode is not selected before inserting the new worksheet(s), 1-2-3 for Windows does not copy the current worksheet's formats and settings to the new worksheet(s).

Headers and Footers

You can include a header and footer when you print your worksheet. The header text, which is printed on the first line after the top margin, is followed by two blank header lines preceding the report. The footer text is printed above the bottom margin and below two blank footer lines.

To create a custom header or footer
1 Choose **F**ile Pa**g**e Setup. The Page Setup dialog box appears.

A header or footer can have three parts; boxes are provided for each of these three parts in the Page Setup dialog box. Whatever you enter in the first box is aligned at the left margin; the text in the second box is centered between the left and right margins; the text in the third box is aligned at the right margin.

2 Place the cursor in the appropriate box (left-aligned, centered, or right-aligned) next to **H**eader or **F**ooter.

The insert icons become active immediately. In addition to any text you enter, the header or footer can include codes for inserting page numbers, the date or time of printing, the file name, or the contents of a cell. Specify the codes you want to use from the following list:

Insert Icon	Code	Description
	@	Inserts the date
	+	Inserts the time
	#	Inserts the page number
	^	Inserts the file name
	\	Inserts the contents of a cell

After the \ type the address or range name of the cell that contains the text you want to include in the header or footer. The specified cell address or range name can contain a formula. If you specify a range name, 1-2-3 for Windows uses the contents of only the first cell in the range.

3 Choose OK.

To change or delete a header or footer

1 Choose **F**ile Pa**g**e Setup. The Page Setup dialog box appears.

2 Edit the contents of the **H**eader or **F**ooter text boxes, or delete the contents.

3 Choose OK.

Help

1-2-3 for Windows provides on-line, context-sensitive help at the touch of a key. You can be in the middle of any operation and press F1 (Help) to display one or more screens of explanations and advice on what to do next. To display the **H**elp menu, choose **H**elp from the menu bar or press F1. Then choose the **C**ontents command. Click the large icon for the general Help topic you want.

The Help utility appears in a window that you can move and size like any other window. To move back and forth among windows, click the window you want to work in or press Alt+Tab. You may want to continue displaying the Help window while you work in 1-2-3; if so, choose the Always on **T**op command from the **H**elp menu in the Help window.

Certain Help topics appear in a color, usually green, or intensity different from that of the rest of the Help window. If you place the mouse pointer on a colored topic, the pointer changes from an arrow to a hand with a pointing index finger. To see more information about one of these topics, click that topic.

The 1-2-3 Help utility conforms to Windows Help standards. You can jump to the contents page, for example, by clicking the **C**ontents button. The **S**earch button displays a dialog box enabling you to type a word for the topic you want to see. The His**t**ory button moves backward through the topics you already viewed; the **B**ack button moves to the last topic you viewed. You can browse through all Help windows in order by clicking the >> and << buttons to move forward or backward, respectively, through the windows.

The Help utility also provides several useful menu commands. Two of the most useful commands are **F**ile **P**rint Topic and **E**dit **C**opy. The first command prints the text of the current Help topic; the second copies all or part of the topic to the Windows Clipboard.

1-2-3 for Windows features a 30-minute on-line animated Guided Tour, which introduces charting, databases, drawing, macros, and other features. The Guided Tour is run from Windows Program Manager; click the Guided Tour icon in the Lotus 1-2-3 Release 5 application group. To learn 1-2-3 by practicing eight hands-on lessons, choose **H**elp **T**utorial. You can choose which lesson you want, or complete each one in sequence.

Hiding Data

See *Protecting Files and Data*

Importing Data

Lotus provides several means of importing data from other applications. The Translate utility has options that convert data directly to 1-2-3 for Windows worksheets from dBASE, Excel, Paradox, and other file formats. You then can access the data by using the **F**ile **O**pen command from the current worksheet.

To import data from a text file

1 Choose **F**ile **O**pen. The Open File dialog box appears.

Shortcut
Click the Open File SmartIcon.

2 Select Text(txt;prn;csv;dat;out;asc) from the File **T**ype list box.

3 Locate the directory where the text file is stored, then enter the file name in the File **N**ame text box.

4 Select **T**ext Options to display the Text Options dialog box. Depending on the format, text files can be read directly into a range or column of cells.

Importing Data **113**

5 In the Bring Into Columns Based On area, select an option button:

- **S**eparator tells 1-2-3 to break the text into columns in the worksheet when a particular character is encountered in the text file. If you select Other Character, a text box appears for entry of a character you specify.

- **L**ayout of File allows 1-2-3 to select where to break into columns based on breaks in the text file.

- **P**ut Everything in One Column imports the data in the text file into a single worksheet column.

6 In the **C**haracter Set text box, select the code page you want 1-2-3 to use to translate the data in the text file. Windows ANSI or DOS are the probable choices.

7 Choose OK to close the Text Options dialog box, then choose OK in the Open File dialog box to import the file.

You also can use certain macro commands to read and write an ASCII sequential file directly from within a 1-2-3 for Windows macro command program.

To import data from an Excel worksheet

1 Choose **F**ile **O**pen. The Open File dialog box appears.

> **Shortcut**
>
> Click the Open File SmartIcon.

2 Select Excel(xls;xlt;xlw) from the File **T**ype list box.

3 Locate the directory where the Excel workbook is stored, then enter the file name in the File **N**ame text box.

4 Choose OK. The workbook is imported into 1-2-3 for Windows.

Inserting Rows, Columns, and Worksheets

Just as you can delete rows, columns, and worksheets, you can insert them anywhere in the worksheet file with the **E**dit **I**nsert command.

To insert rows, columns, or worksheets

1 Choose **E**dit **I**nsert. The Worksheet Insert dialog box appears.

2 Choose what dimension to insert (**C**olumn, **R**ow, or **S**heet).

> **Shortcut**
>
> 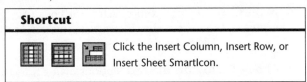 Click the Insert Column, Insert Row, or Insert Sheet SmartIcon.

Another method of inserting is to highlight the rows, columns, or worksheet, then press Ctrl+ gray +. Lotus refers to the + key on the numeric keypad as the *gray +*.

When you insert rows, all rows below the cell pointer move down. When you insert columns, all columns to the right of the cell pointer move to the right. When you insert worksheets, all the worksheets behind the new ones receive new worksheet letters. For example, if you insert a new worksheet after worksheet A, and worksheet B already exists, the new worksheet becomes B, the former worksheet B becomes worksheet C, and so on. All addresses and formulas adjust automatically.

If Group mode is activated, and you insert columns or rows, those changes are reflected in every worksheet in the file.

If you insert a row or column within the borders of a range, the range expands to accommodate the new rows or columns. If you insert a worksheet within a range that spans worksheets, the range expands automatically to accommodate the new worksheet. Formulas referring to that range include the new cells.

Installing 1-2-3 for Windows

Installing 1-2-3 Release 5 for Windows is simple. Just start the Install program, and follow the on-screen instructions. You must install this software on a hard disk.

To install 1-2-3 for Windows

1 Start Microsoft Windows, and place the Install disk in drive A. (If you install from a different drive, substitute that drive's letter.)

2 Choose File Run from the Program Manager menu, and type **A:INSTALL** in the Command Line text box.

3 Choose OK. An on-screen message informs you that Install is initializing, then the Welcome to Install screen appears.

The 1-2-3 for Windows Install program appears as a series of dialog boxes. If you need help at any time during installation, select the Help button in the dialog box.

4 Enter your name and company in the Your Name and Company Name text boxes. Choose Next, and then Yes to confirm.

5 Install then informs you that it wants to move shared files. Choose OK. The Installation Method & Program Directory dialog box appears.

6 Choose an installation method option button based on the description in the dialog box.

If you choose Customize features, Install will present a dialog box for selection of each feature you want to install.

7 In the **1**-2-3 Program Directory text box, enter the directory where you want to install 1-2-3 or keep the default that is suggested. Choose Next.

116 Installing 1-2-3 for Windows

8 In the Select Program Group dialog box, select the Program Group for the 1-2-3 application icons. Choose **N**ext.

9 Choose **Y**es to begin copying files to your hard disk. Or choose E**x**it Install if you don't want to install 1-2-3 now.

Left Align

By default, 1-2-3 for Windows aligns labels to the left and values (numbers and formulas) to the right of the cell. You can align values to the left, if desired, without affecting use of the cells in calculations.

Entries will be left-aligned if you start by typing the ' prefix. You can also left-align data you have already entered data in cells.

To align data

1 Highlight the range and then choose **S**tyle **A**lignment. The Alignment dialog box appears.

2 In the Horizontal area of the Alignment dialog box, select the **L**eft option button.

Shortcut
Press Ctrl+L
or
Click the Left Align SmartIcon.

3 Choose OK.

Lines and Colors

The Lines & Color dialog box enables you to enhance and emphasize data in a worksheet by choosing colors, specifying borders, and adding frames.

To add lines and colors

1 Choose **S**tyle **L**ines & Color. The Lines & Color dialog box appears.

> **Shortcut**
>
> Click the Lines & Color SmartIcon.

2 Just under the **C**ancel button, the Sample box shows how the choices you make in the Lines & Color dialog box will appear in the worksheet. Refer to the Sample box as you experiment with different colors, patterns, borders, and frames before actually applying them to the selected range. When you are satisfied with the choices you have made, click OK.

The settings in the Interior area of the Lines & Color dialog box enable you to specify a **B**ackground Color, **P**attern, Pattern **C**olor, and Te**x**t Color for any cells or ranges in the worksheet. You can display negative numbers in red by clicking on the Negative **V**alues in Red check box.

Use the settings in the Border section of the Lines & Color dialog box to draw lines above, below, on the sides of, and around cells in a range. To outline all cells in a selected range (as if they were one object), choose **O**utline. To outline individual cells in the selected range, choose A**l**l. Choose a style and color for the border from the Line St**y**le and Li**n**e Color drop-down boxes.

To further enhance borders, you can click the **D**esigner Frame check box to choose from a collection of specially designed frames. After you choose a frame style, choose a color from the **F**rame Color drop-down list. See also, *Borders*.

Linking Applications

Using **E**dit **C**opy and **E**dit **P**aste to transfer data from one Windows application to another does not set up a link between the original and the copy. Without a link, you can change either version without affecting the other. To establish a link, you must use a special capability of some Windows applications called *object linking and embedding* (OLE). All Lotus Windows applications can take full advantage of OLE.

Lotus recommends that you include in the PATH statement of your computer's AUTOEXEC.BAT file the full paths to the applications you use when linking and embedding data.

When you copy an object by using *object linking*, the data for the object resides in the file in which it was originally created. If you use object linking to copy a table of numbers from 1-2-3 to Ami Pro, for example, the data remains in 1-2-3 but a "picture" of it exists in Ami Pro also. To change the picture in Ami Pro, you return to 1-2-3 and change the original numbers. (Windows makes switching between applications easy: to return to the application in which an object originally was created, simply double-click the object.)

When you copy an object by using *object embedding*, the data for the object is copied to the destination application. Because it resides there rather than only in the original application, you can move the file with the embedded data to another computer. When you take a file with embedded data to a different computer, you don't have to take all the files in which the original data is stored (as you would with object linking). As long as the computer to which you move the file has a copy of the same application you used to create the embedded data, you can use that application's facilities to edit the embedded data.

When an object is embedded in another application, any edits you make to the object in the original application are not reflected in the embedded copy.

Whether you use object linking or object embedding depends on several factors. If you have to give to someone else a document that contains objects from several applications, embed the objects. Only if the objects are embedded is their data stored in the file you give. The result is a larger file than if you had used object linking, but having the data available in the file is well worth the cost in disk space. If the document is to remain on your PC, however, and your prime concern is simply setting up a system that automatically updates the copies of objects if you update the originals, use object linking.

To link data

1 Create the object. Be sure to save the file before continuing. An object to be linked must be stored in a saved file in its original application.

2 Select the object to be linked by clicking on it.

3 From the **E**dit menu, select **C**opy. This action places a copy of the object on the Windows Clipboard.

To see the object on the Clipboard, open a Windows accessory called Clipboard Viewer. (It's in the Accessories group of the Windows Program Manager.)

4 Switch to the second application, and position the pointer where the linked object should appear in that application.

5 From the **E**dit menu of the second application, select Paste Lin**k**. (In some applications, you choose Paste Special, and then select the Paste Link option located in a dialog box.)

After you link an object, you can switch to the original application, make a change to the object, and see the revision also appear in the second application. The revision appears only if Automatic Updating is turned on. If Manual Updating is on instead, you must use the Update command in the second application to update a link.

To edit an object that has been linked, you do not need to manually switch to the application that created the object and then load and edit the object. You can simply double-click the object in the application to which it has been linked. When you double-click a linked object, Windows automatically opens the application used to create the object and loads the file with the data for the object.

If you have updated data linked to a second 1-2-3 for Windows worksheet that is currently not open, the linked data will be updated automatically when you open the second worksheet.

To embed an object

You have several ways to embed an object from one application into another. One way is to use the Insert **O**bject command from within an application. Follow these steps:

1 Position the pointer in the application where the object should appear.

2 Choose Insert **O**bject from the **E**dit menu.

> **Shortcut**
>
> Click the Embed Data SmartIcon.

3 A dialog box appears, listing all the available object types. The types listed are determined by the applications in your system that can provide objects for embedding. The more applications you have, the more object types you see on the list.

From the list of object types, select a type. The application that creates objects of that type opens so that you can make the object you need.

4 Create the object using the tools of the second application.

5 When finished, select E**x**it & Return. The second application closes and you return to the original application with the newly created object in place.

With this method of embedding, you visit a second application just long enough to create an object expressly for use in the first application. The data for the object is stored in the first application along with information about which application created the object.

To edit the object, you can double-click on it just as you double-click a linked object. The application used to create the object reopens, with the object on-screen and ready for editing.

If you want to embed an object already created in another application, follow these steps to get the same results as the preceding method:

1 Select the object.

2 Copy it to the Windows Clipboard.

3 Switch to a second application.

4 Select Edit Paste Special. The Paste Special dialog box appears.

5 Select the object you just created from the list of available data on the Clipboard. Be sure to select the item referred to as an "object."

6 Click the **P**aste button.

Macros

Macros are text labels that automate the same keystrokes you enter while using 1-2-3 for Windows. The simplest type of macro is nothing more than a short collection of keystrokes that 1-2-3 for Windows enters into the worksheet for you. Because the program stores this keystroke collection as text in a cell, you can treat the text as you would any label.

Consider the number of times you save and retrieve worksheet files, print reports, and set and reset worksheet formats. In each case, you perform the operation by typing a series of keystrokes—sometimes a rather long series. By running a macro, however, you can reduce any number of keystrokes to a two-keystroke abbreviation.

Creating Macros

Enter macros in three columns of a worksheet: one column for the macro's name, one column for the macro code, and one column to explain each line of the macro code. In addition to entering macros manually, you can use the Transcript window to record macros (see "Recording Macros").

Good planning and documentation are important for creating macros that run smoothly and efficiently. Regardless of your level of expertise with macros, you should always follow seven basic steps.

To create a macro

1 *Plan what you want the macro to do.* Write down all the tasks you want the macro to perform; then arrange those tasks in the order in which they must be completed.

2 *Identify the keystrokes or commands the macro must use.* Keep in mind that macros can be as simple as labels (text) that duplicate the keystrokes you want to replay.

3 *Find an area of the worksheet in which you can enter macros.* If you choose the worksheet area, consider that executed macros read text from cells, starting with the top cell and working down through lower cells. Macros end if they encounter a blank cell, a cell with a numeric value, or a command that stops a macro's execution. Enter macro code, therefore, as labels in successive cells in the same column.

4 *Use the correct syntax to enter the keystrokes and macro commands into a cell or cells.* You can enter macros manually or copy recorded keystrokes from the Transcript window.

5 *Name the macro.* You can name a macro (by using the **R**ange **N**ame command) in one of three ways:

- Assign the macro a Ctrl+*letter* name. This type of name consists of a backslash (\) followed by an alphabetic character (for example, \a).

- Choose a descriptive name of up to 15 letters, numbers, and underscores, such as PRINT_BUDGET.

- Give the name \0 (backslash zero) to a macro if you want that macro to run automatically when the file is loaded. The Run Autoexecute **M**acros check box in the User Setup dialog box enables you to disable and re-enable the auto-execute feature of macros named \0.

6 *Document the macro.* To facilitate the editing and debugging process, you can document a macro in several ways:

- Use a descriptive macro name, and consistently use range names instead of cell addresses in macros. Addresses entered in the text of a macro are not updated if changes are made to the worksheet. Range names in a macro, however, *are* updated if the worksheet changes.

- Include comments as a separate column to the right of the actual macro code within the worksheet.

- Retain all the paperwork you used to design and construct the macro for later reference.

7 *Test and debug the macro.* Even if you have a good design and thorough documentation, plan to test and debug your macros. Testing enables you to verify that a macro works precisely as you want it to. If necessary, you must debug the macro to remove such problems as spelling or typing mistakes and syntax errors.

Recording Macros

The Transcript window can record keystrokes and mouse movements as macro commands while you are in a 1-2-3 for Windows session. You can copy these recorded macros as labels into worksheet cells so that you can use or edit the macros.

To record a macro

1 Choose **T**ools **M**acro Show Tra**n**script to display the Transcript window as it records commands.

Shortcut
Click the Transcript Window SmartIcon.

2 To begin recording a macro in the Transcript window, select **T**ools **M**acro Re**c**ord. Then press the keys you want to include in the macro.

Shortcut
Click the Record Macro SmartIcon.

3 Stop recording the macro by selecting **T**ools **M**acro Stop Re**c**ording or by clicking the Record Macro SmartIcon again.

The following figure shows the Transcript window after text was entered into the worksheet, the size of the type was modified, and a background pattern and border were added.

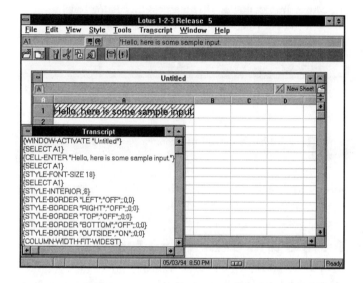

You enter recorded commands into the worksheet by copying them from the Transcript window to the Clipboard and then pasting them into the worksheet.

Running Macros

You can start macros in several different ways, depending on how the macros are named. Consider the following examples:

- Execute a macro named with the backslash (\) and a letter by holding the Ctrl key and pressing the designated letter of the alphabet.

- Execute a macro with a descriptive name of up to 15 characters by using the Macro Run dialog box.

- An auto-execute macro (one with the name \0) runs whenever a file containing the \0 macro is loaded—if the Run Autoexecute **M**acros check box is selected in the User Setup dialog box.

To run a macro

You can execute any macro, even if it has no name, by using the Macro Run dialog box. You access this dialog box by choosing **T**ools **M**acro **R**un from the 1-2-3 for Windows menu.

Shortcut
Press Alt+F3 (Run).
or
Click the Run Macro SmartIcon.

Specify the macro's first cell as the address in the **M**acro Name text box, and then click OK.

Testing and Debugging Macros

1-2-3 for Windows provides two valuable aids to help you verify a macro's operation and locate macro errors: Single Step and Trace modes. *Single Step mode* enables you to execute the macro one keystroke at a time. This mode enables you to see, one instruction at a time, exactly what the macro does. *Trace mode* opens a small window that shows the macro instruction being executed and the cell location of that instruction.

Single Step and Trace are independent features, but they work well together. You can watch and analyze the macro action within the worksheet by using Single Step mode; the Macro Trace window indicates which macro instruction is being executed. Without these tools, macros often execute too rapidly for you to see the problem areas.

To test and debug a macro

1. Choose **T**ools **M**acro **T**race. The Macro Trace window appears.

   > **Shortcut**
   >
   > Click the Trace Mode SmartIcon.

2. Choose **T**ools **M**acro **S**ingle Step. This action instructs 1-2-3 for Windows to execute macros one instruction at a time.

   > **Shortcut**
   >
   > Press Alt+F2 (Step) to toggle Single Step mode.
   >
   > or
   >
   > Click the Step Mode SmartIcon.

3. Start the macro you want to step through one keystroke at a time. After the macro starts, the <Location> and <Instructions> place markers in the Macro Trace window are replaced by cell addresses and the macro code, respectively.

4. Press any key to begin macro operation. The Macro Trace window highlights the macro instruction being executed and identifies the cell containing that instruction.

5. Execute each step in sequence by pressing any key after each subsequent step. Pressing a key instructs 1-2-3 for Windows to perform the next step of the macro.

6. If you find an error, terminate the macro by pressing Ctrl+Break; then press Esc or Enter. Edit the macro to correct the error. Then repeat the test procedure in case other errors exist in the macro.

Translating 1-2-3 for Windows Release 1.*x* Macros

Before you can use 1-2-3 Release 1.*x* for Windows macros in 1-2-3 Release 5 for Windows, you must use the 1-2-3 Macro Translator to perform a one-time translation of your Release 1.*x* macros. You do not need to translate macros created with Releases 2.x, 3.x, or 4.x of 1-2-3.

The 1-2-3 Macro Translator is installed in the same Windows program group as 1-2-3 Release 5 for Windows. You run the 1-2-3 Macro Translator as a separate program.

To translate Release 1.*x* macros

1 Double-click the 1-2-3 Macro Translator icon in the Windows Program Manager. The 1-2-3 for Windows Macro Translator dialog box appears.

2 Choose the files to translate, and then select the **T**ranslate button. If you do not specify a new destination directory, the 1-2-3 Macro Translator warns you that it will back up the originals. Select Yes to continue.

3 After the 1-2-3 Macro Translator translates the files, it informs you of the number of files it translated. Click OK to return to the program.

4 After you translate all the files you need converted to Release 5, select E**x**it to leave the Translator.

Using Macro Buttons

A *macro button* is a button that executes an associated macro after you click that button. You can add a macro button to a worksheet to make it easier to perform certain tasks for which you have recorded or written macros. Macro buttons always appear at the same location on a worksheet (unless you choose to move the button, as explained later in this section). That is, after you create a macro button, the button scrolls along with the cells it covers.

To create a macro button

1. Choose **T**ools **D**raw **B**utton. The pointer changes from an arrow to a crosshair.

Shortcut
Click the Macro Button SmartIcon.

2. Point to the worksheet location where you want to place the macro button.

3. To create a button of the default size, click the left mouse button. To create a macro button in a different size (perhaps to provide room for more text on the button's face), drag the mouse pointer until the dotted button box is the desired size.

   After you release the mouse button, the Assign to Button dialog box appears.

4. If the macro you want to assign to the button is short, enter the macro text in the **E**nter Macro Here text box.

   To enter the address of a range containing a macro that already exists, choose the **A**ssign Macro From list box, and select Range.

   Enter the address of the existing macro in the **R**ange text box, or select the name of the macro from the Existing **N**amed Ranges list box.

5. Change the text on the face of the button to show the button's purpose by typing the new description in the **B**utton Text text box.

6. Click OK to return to the worksheet.

To modify a macro button

To move or resize a macro button—or to modify its actions—you first must select the macro button by holding either the Shift or Ctrl key before clicking the macro button. After you select a macro button, the button is surrounded by eight rectangular handles. You can perform the following operations to a selected macro button:

- To resize a selected button, drag one of the handles until the button is the correct size.

- To move a selected button, drag the button to the new location.

- To edit the button's text or to change the macro assigned to the button, double-click the selected button. Then use the options in the Assign to Button dialog box to make the desired changes.

Using Macro Commands

All 1-2-3 for Windows macro commands are enclosed in braces ({}). The braces tell 1-2-3 for Windows where a macro command begins and ends. Some macro commands are a single command enclosed in braces, while many other macro commands have *arguments*, or parameters, after the command, within the braces.

To view an on-screen listing of macro commands

1 Type { (open brace).

2 Press F3 (Name). The Macro Keywords dialog box appears.

3 Highlight the name of the desired macro command.

4 To see a description of the macro command, press F1 (Help) or click the **?** button.

5 Click OK to enter the macro command in the current cell.

> **Shortcut**
>
> Click the Select Macro Command SmartIcon.

Release 5 has introduced more new macro commands, including macros to assign printer setup settings such as page size, orientation, and number of copies. Refer to *Using 1-2-3 Release 5 for Windows*, Special Edition, for a detailed explanation of each macro command.

Mapping

Maps are a special chart format now available with 1-2-3 Release 5 for Windows. You can embed a map linked to worksheet data, displaying various colors and patterns representing data for states, provinces, countries, or grouped regions.

The maps available are: World Countries, USA by State, Canada by Province, Alaska, Europe, Japan, Hawaii, Mexico, Australia, and Taiwan. The region names or codes you enter in the worksheet determine which map type is created. If your worksheet range contains names or codes for states, for example, the USA map appears.

1-2-3 groups the data in the map data range into up to 12 categories. You can change the colors and patterns used for the categories, and use pin characters to mark locations, such as cities.

After you create a map, the Map Viewer enables you to zoom in on areas of the map and further customize the map.

To create a map

1 Create a data range from which the map will be drawn.

- The first column of the range must contain geographic region names or map codes. For a map of the United States, the codes happen to correspond to the two-character postal abbreviations.

> **Note**
>
> For a list of map codes for countries or states, choose **H**elp **S**earch, select the word Maps, then select the topic Countries of the World Map Codes or USA by State Map Codes. You can choose **E**dit **C**opy in the Help window to display the Copy dialog box. Highlight the names and codes you want to copy and then choose the **C**opy button to copy them to the Clipboard. When you return to the worksheet, choose **E**dit **P**aste to paste the names into the worksheet.

- The second column of the data range contains data that you want to chart on the map as colors, patterns, or pin characters. Colors are assigned automatically, but can be edited after you create the map.

- (Optional) The third column can contain another kind of information, such as region names, allowing regions to be marked with patterns, while the components of the region are individually colored based on the data values.

- (Optional) The third or fourth column can contain pin characters for any of the geographic areas that you want to mark, such as important cities. These symbols can be characters such as those in the Zapf Dingbat or Wingdings fonts.

2 Highlight the data range.

3 Choose **T**ools Ma**p I**nsert Map Object. The mouse pointer becomes a crosshair with a globe.

If the Map Type dialog box appears, select a map name, and then choose OK.

Mapping **133**

> **Shortcut**
>
> Click the Create Map SmartIcon.

4 Click the worksheet where you want to place the top left corner of the map. The map appears with selection handles, and can be resized and moved.

> **Note**
>
> If 1-2-3 does not recognize a geographic code in the range, the Region Check dialog box appears, showing the unknown region label. In the **K**nown Map Region list box, select the correct name or code. You can add the unknown map region as a custom name for a known map region by selecting the **A**dd As Custom Name For option button.

The following figure shows a map and the data range on which it is based.

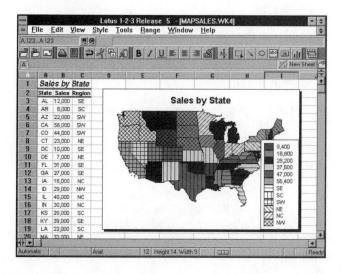

134 Mapping

To change the map color and pattern settings

1. Click the map to select it (if it is not already selected). Selection handles appear on the border.

2. Choose **T**ools Ma**p** **C**olor Settings. The Color Settings dialog box appears. This dialog box enables you to change the settings 1-2-3 assigned based on the data values in the second column of the map data range.

   The default setting for **V**alues, **L**egend Labels, and **C**olors is Automatic. Clicking the corresponding drop-down list enables you to select Manual (to edit each bin) or From Range (to specify a range of data).

3. In the **V**alues drop-down list, select Manual. Change the values in the bins to set new upper limits, if necessary.

   The map regions that have values within a bin's limits are displayed using the color assigned to that bin. To display only exact matches for the data entered in the bins, click the **E**xact match option button.

   The legend labels automatically change to match the entries in the Values area. To manually change the labels displayed in the map legend, choose the **L**egend Labels drop-down box. Select Manual, and then edit the bin settings.

4. In the **C**olors drop-down list, select Manual. For any (or each) of the six bins, click the drop-down color palette, and then click a new color for that bin.

5. Choose OK. Changes to the color settings are applied to the map.

You can change the pattern settings in the same way that you change the color settings. Choose **T**ools Ma**p** **P**attern Settings, and then refer to the steps above, changing patterns instead of colors.

Mapping **135**

To change the map ranges and title

1. Click the map to select it (if it is not already selected). Selection handles appear on the border.

2. Choose **T**ools Ma**p** Ranges & **T**itle to display the Ranges & Title dialog box.

3. In the **A**ssign Range For list box, select the feature for which you want to change the range. The currently selected range address appears in the Range text box.

4. Type a different range in the **R**ange text box, or click the range selector button to highlight the range.

5. Repeat steps 3 and 4 to change ranges for the other features.

6. In the **T**itle text box, type a new title for the map. If you prefer to link the map title to a cell in the worksheet, click the Cell check box, and then enter the range of the title in the Title text box.

Maps can be enhanced with text blocks or other drawn objects to customize for presentations. You can also use the Map Viewer to take a close look at the map you created and make other changes.

To use the Map Viewer

1. Double-click the map. The Lotus Map Viewer window appears.

2. Try some of the following features available in the Map Viewer:

   - Click the Maximize button in the upper right corner of the window to view the map full screen.

   - Move the mouse pointer over the map. The state or country abbreviation appears in the status bar.

   - Zoom in on an area of the map by clicking and dragging the mouse to outline the area to enlarge. Choose **V**iew **R**eset to change the size to normal.

- You can also choose **V**iew **Z**oom In and **V**iew Zoom **O**ut to view the map in various magnifications.

- To change the font and attributes of the title or the legend text, click the right mouse button on the object, then click Font and Attributes. The Font dialog box appears. Modify the settings and then choose OK to view the changes.

- Change the location of the title or legend by clicking the object, then dragging to a new location.

- To copy the code, name, or coordinates of a state or country, to paste them to the worksheet, place the mouse pointer on the state or country, then click the right mouse button. On the quick menu that appears, choose Copy Region Code, Copy Region Name, or Copy Region Coordinates. The data appears in the status bar and is copied to the Clipboard.

- Choose **E**dit **C**opy to copy the contents of the window to the Clipboard, for linking or embedding in another application.

- To add an overlay to the map—for example, to display Canada with the United States map—choose **M**ap **A**dd Overlay. The Add Overlay dialog box appears. Change to the \123R5W\MAPDATA directory. Choose from the .tv files in the File **N**ame list box—for example, `canada.tv`. Choose OK. The overlay appears on the map.

- You can add more than one overlay to the map by choosing the **M**ap **A**dd Overlay command repeatedly. To remove any of the overlays, choose Map R**e**move Overlay.

3 Choose **F**ile **U**pdate to update the map embedded in the worksheet with the changes you have made. (Skip this step to avoid saving the changes you made in the Map Viewer window.)

4 Choose **F**ile E**x**it & Return to close the Map Viewer and return to the worksheet.

Margins

By default, 1-2-3 for Windows creates a 0.5-inch margin on the top, bottom, left, and right sides of the page. If your report has a header, it will appear after (not within) the top margin, and footer text appears above the bottom margin. If you didn't specify a header, the report begins printing immediately after the top margin.

To change the margins

1 Choose **F**ile Pa**g**e Setup. The Page Setup dialog box appears.

Shortcut
Click the Page Setup SmartIcon.

2 In the Margins area of the dialog box, edit the setting in the **T**op, **B**ottom, **L**eft, or **R**ight text boxes.

3 Choose OK.

Matrices

The **R**ange **A**nalyze **I**nvert Matrix and **R**ange **A**nalyze **M**ultiply Matrix commands are specialized mathematical commands that enable you to solve systems of simultaneous linear equations and manipulate the resulting solutions. If you are using 1-2-3 for Windows for certain types of economic analysis or for scientific or engineering calculations, you may find these commands valuable.

The **R**ange **A**nalyze **I**nvert Matrix command enables you to invert a nonsingular square matrix of up to 80 rows and columns. The **R**ange **A**nalyze **M**ultiply Matrix command enables you to multiply two rectangular matrices together in accordance with the rules of matrix algebra. The number of columns in the first matrix must equal the number of rows in the second matrix. The result matrix has the same number of rows as the first matrix, and the same number of columns as the second.

To invert/multiply a matrix

1. Choose Range **A**nalyze **I**nvert Matrix. The Invert Matrix dialog box appears.

2. Specify the **F**rom matrix and the **T**o matrix.

3. Choose OK.

4. Choose **R**ange **A**nalyze **M**ultiply Matrix. The Multiply Matrix dialog box appears.

5. Specify the **F**irst Matrix, the **S**econd Matrix, and the **R**esulting Matrix.

6. Choose OK.

Inverting and multiplying matrices can be time-consuming, especially when you are dealing with large matrices or your system lacks a numeric coprocessor.

Menus

The 1-2-3 for Windows main menu changes to reflect the current selection. If you're working with a range, for example, the main menu displays the **R**ange command.

1-2-3 Release 5 also provides *quick menus*, which appear after you click the right mouse button. These menus contain frequently used commands that you can use with the current selection.

In addition to the 1-2-3 for Windows main menu, the program also offers the *1-2-3 Classic* menu, which includes the 1-2-3 and WYSIWYG menus from 1-2-3 for DOS Release 3.1. To access the 1-2-3 Classic menu, type /. The 1-2-3 Classic menu enables you to use existing 1-2-3 macros and to continue using command sequences you already know as you learn 1-2-3 for Windows. Discussions in this book focus on using the 1-2-3 for Windows menu instead of the 1-2-3 Classic menu.

You can use both the mouse and the keyboard to select commands. With some commands, a dialog box appears with additional options. You can select the options you want and choose OK to execute the command.

To select a command with the mouse

1 Click the menu name. A list of menu commands drops down.

2 Click the command you want.

3 If a dialog box appears, make the selections you want. Different dialog boxes contain different elements. Following are the most common elements, as well as how to make a selection:

Element	Action
List box	Click the item you want in the list box.
Option buttons	Click the option button. When an option is selected, the button is darkened in the center. When the option is not selected, the button is blank. You can select only one option in each group of options.
Check Boxes	Click the check box. When a check box is activated, an X appears. When a check box is not selected, it is blank. You can select more than one check box in a group of check boxes.

(continues)

Element	Action
Tab	Click the tab.
Text box	Click the text box; then delete and retype the entry or edit the entry.
Spin box	Type your own entry or click the up spin arrow to increase the value or click the down spin arrow to decrease the value.
Drop-down list box	Click the arrow next to the option name to display the drop-down list. Then click the list item you want.
Command buttons	Click the button you want. Clicking OK confirms the selections. Clicking Cancel closes the dialog box without making the changes.

> **Tip**
>
> Use the SmartIcons for quick access to certain commands. See *SmartIcons*.

To display quick menus

1 Select the items you want to modify. Depending on what you select, the quick menu will vary. Therefore, select what you want to work with first.

2 Press the right mouse button. A quick menu of options that pertain to the selection appears.

3 Select an option by clicking it, or highlight it using the direction keys and then press Enter.

To select a command with the keyboard

1 Press Alt+*the underlined key letter* of the menu. The key letter is underlined on-screen.

2 Press the key letter of the command, or press the down-arrow key to move to the command you want, and then press Enter.

3 If a dialog box appears, make the selections you want. Different dialog boxes contain different elements. Following are the most common elements, as well as how to make a selection:

Element	Action
Tab	Press Ctrl+Tab or use the arrow keys to move to the next tab; press Ctrl+Shift+Tab to move to the previous tab.
List box	Press Alt+*the key letter* to select the list box. Use the arrow keys to select the item in the list, and then press Enter.
Option buttons	Press Alt+*the key letter* to select the option button.
Check boxes	Press Alt+*the key letter* to select the check box.
Text box	Press Alt+*the key letter* to select the text box. Type your entry.
Spin box	Press Alt+*the key letter* to select the spin box. Type your entry or press ↑ to increase the value or press ↓ to decrease the value.
Drop-down list box	Press Alt+*the key letter* to display the list box. Use the arrow keys to select the item you want, and then press Enter.
Command buttons	Press Enter to choose the OK button. Press Esc to choose the Cancel Button. To choose any other button, press Alt+*the key letter*.

> **Shortcut**
>
> Choose **E**dit **U**ndo or press Ctrl+Z to undo a command
>
> or
>
> Click the Undo SmartIcon.

See *Navigating the Worksheet* for information on using the mouse or keyboard shortcuts to select commands.

Moving Data

In a move operation, the data being moved or copied is called the *source* and the location to which you are moving the data is called the *target* or *destination*. When you move data, the source data disappears from its original location and reappears at the target location.

If the destination range contains data, that data will be replaced by the data you move unless the destination cells are protected. Be sure to specify a destination large enough to contain the source data.

Remember that you can use the **E**dit **U**ndo command, press Ctrl+Z (Undo), or click the Undo SmartIcon to correct a mistake in moving a range.

To drag a range to a new location

1. Highlight the desired range you want to move.

2. Click the mouse near one edge of the range and drag to another location in the same worksheet. When you move the mouse pointer to the edge of the highlighted range, the pointer changes into a hand. You can use this technique to move a single cell or a range of cells. However, you cannot drag a collection with the mouse.

To drag-and-drop across the worksheet

You may want to move the data to a distant area in the worksheet, or to a separate sheet in the worksheet. You can still use drag-and-drop if you first window the two areas.

1 Choose **V**iew **S**plit. The sheet splits into two windows.

2 In one of the windows, scroll to display the range to be moved.

3 In the other window, click a sheet tab or the New Sheet button if the data is to be moved to another sheet. Scroll to the area of the sheet where the data will be moved.

4 Highlight the cell or range you want to move.

5 Next, move the mouse pointer to any edge of the selection (until the mouse pointer changes to a hand).

6 Click and drag the selection to its new location in the other window. When you reach the destination, release the mouse button.

If you try to drop the range in an area that already has data, 1-2-3 for Windows asks you if it is OK to replace the data. Choose OK to replace the data, or Cancel to avoid overwriting the data.

To drag-and-drop across files

1 Open the source file and the file to which you want to move data, the destination file.

2 Choose **W**indow **T**ile to display the files side by side. Scroll each window to make the source and destination areas visible.

3 Highlight the cell or range you want to move.

4 Next, move the mouse pointer to any edge of the selection (until the mouse pointer changes to a hand).

5 Click and drag the selection to its new location in the other window. When you reach the destination, release the mouse button.

When you drag-and-drop to another file, the range remains in the original file; you have created a copy. If you do not want the range to exist in the original file, you must delete it after the drag-and-drop operation.

To cut and paste a range

To move data by cutting and pasting, you *cut* the data from the worksheet to the Clipboard, a Windows holding area in memory. Then you *paste* the data from the Clipboard to a new location in the worksheet, to a different worksheet in the same file, to a different file, or to a different Windows 3.x application. You can move entire columns, rows, or worksheets with this method, but you cannot move a column to a row, a row to a column, or a worksheet or file to a column or row.

You can use paste many times to copy the same information to many different locations. If you want to copy data to many different places, however, do not interrupt your pasting operations by cutting or copying other data to the Clipboard. Only the contents of the most recent copy or cut operation can be stored on the Clipboard.

To cut and paste data, follow these steps:

1 Highlight the range or cell you want to move.

2 Choose **Edit Cut**.

Shortcut
Press Shift+Del or Ctrl+X.
or
Click the Cut SmartIcon.

3 Move the cell pointer to the first cell of the destination range.

4 Choose **E**dit **P**aste.

Shortcut
Press Shift+Ins or Ctrl+V.
or
Click the Paste SmartIcon.

5 To paste the data in another location, move the cell pointer or select the target range and repeat step 4.

To move styles with Paste Special

Sometimes you want to move the formatting and style attributes of a cell or range to another cell or range. You can do this by selecting the **E**dit Paste **S**pecial command instead of the **E**dit **P**aste command. In the Paste Special dialog box, you have the option of pasting only the styles from the selection. You can also paste the contents without the styles or convert formulas into values when pasting.

Named Styles

One way to assign styles (groups of formats) is to name them. Using a *named style* is especially helpful when a cell or range has several style characteristics attached to it. You can assign names to up to 16 different sets of styles with the Named Style dialog box. Use this dialog box to define styles and apply a style to a selected cell or range.

A named style includes all style characteristics (font, point size, number format, decimal places, color, border, and so on) to be assigned to the selected cell.

To define a named style

1 Select the cell with the format you want to use for a named style.

2 Choose **S**tyle Named **S**tyle. The Named Style dialog box appears.

> **Shortcut**
>
> Click the Named Style SmartIcon.

3 In the **E**xisting Styles list box, choose one of the 16 existing styles. (All undefined styles are identified as #-Undefined, where # is a number between 1 and 16.)

4 In the Style **N**ame text box, enter a name for the style (up to 35 characters).

5 Click the **D**efine button.

6 Choose OK.

To apply a named style

1 Select a range or collection to which you want to apply a named style.

2 Choose **S**tyle Named **S**tyle. The Named Style dialog box appears.

3 Select a style from the Existing Styles list box.

> **Shortcut**
>
> Click the style selector in the status bar.

4 Choose OK. 1-2-3 applies all the attributes of the named style to the cells in the selected range.

To remove a named style

1 Choose **S**tyle Named **S**tyle. The Named Style dialog box appears.

2 Select the style you want to delete from the **E**xisting Styles list box.

3 Choose **C**lear, then choose OK. The named style is removed.

Ranges that use the deleted named style retain the assigned style; however, when you select these ranges, the style selector shows Undefined.

Naming Files

When you create a new file, 1-2-3 automatically assigns the file a temporary file name, FILE*nnnn*.WK4, where *nnnn* is replaced with a number. The first temporary file name is FILE0001.WK4. If you create additional files, 1-2-3 names these files FILE0002.WK4, FILE0003.WK4, and so on, incrementing the numeric portion of the file name with each new file. You can save your work using the temporary file names 1-2-3 assigns, or you can choose a different name.

When you name files, use a descriptive name to help identify your work. Identifying the content of a file named BUDGET93.WK4 is easy, for example, but the file name FILE0001.WK4 doesn't tell you anything about the content of the file.

148 Naming Files

The maximum length of a file name is eight characters. A file name can contain any combination of letters, numbers, hyphens, and underscores. However, with the exception of a single period between the file name and the extension, you cannot use any other special characters, such as spaces, commas, backslashes, or periods.

The standard file extension for 1-2-3 for Windows worksheet files is WK4. When you open or save a file, type only the descriptive part of the name; 1-2-3 for Windows supplies the appropriate file extension for you. 1-2-3 Release 5 for Windows uses the following file extensions.

Extension	Description
AL3	A file in which named page settings are saved.
BAK	A backup copy of a worksheet file.
DB	A Paradox database file.
DBF	A dBASE database file.
FMB	A backup version of a format file (FM3 and FMT extensions). From earlier releases of 1-2-3, a *format file* is a file that stores a worksheet's style information only.
MAC	A macro for a customized icon.
NS4	A 1-2-3 shared file.
TXT	A text file.
WK1	A 1-2-3 for DOS Release 2 worksheet file.
WK3	A 1-2-3 for Windows Release 1 and 1-2-3 for DOS Release 3 worksheet file.
WK4	A 1-2-3 for Windows Release 4 or 5 worksheet file.
WT4	A 1-2-3 SmartMasters worksheet template file.
XLS	An Excel worksheet file.

File extensions help identify the file type. If you use **F**ile **O**pen to open the file BUDGET.WK1, for example, you can tell by the file extension that the file is a 1-2-3 for DOS Release 2 file. 1-2-3 for Windows reads the file from disk and translates the file to WK4 format if you save the file under a new name.

When you choose **F**ile **O**pen, 1-2-3 for Windows lists all the files with extensions beginning with WK. To open a file that has a different extension, select the specific file type in the File **T**ype drop-down list, and then select the file. Alternatively, you can type the complete file name and extension or use wild cards.

Naming Ranges

Range names, which should be descriptive, can include up to 15 characters and can be used in formulas, functions, and commands. You can apply a range name with the **R**ange **N**ame command or the Create/Delete Range Name SmartIcon and view a list of existing range names by using the navigator on the edit line.

The use of range names has a number of advantages. Range names are easier to remember than addresses. Also, using a range name is sometimes faster than pointing to a range in another part of the worksheet. Range names also make formulas easier to understand.

Whenever 1-2-3 for Windows expects the address of a cell or range, you can specify a range name. Two ways to specify a range name are available. You can type the range name in the dialog box, or you can click the navigator on the edit line to display a list of range names. The navigator lists the range names in alphabetical order. Click the name you want.

Because a single cell is considered a valid range, you can name a single cell as a range. If a command or action, such as GoTo (F5), calls for a single cell address, you can specify the cell by typing its range name. If you type a range name that applies to a multiple-cell range in this case, 1-2-3 for Windows uses the upper left corner of the range.

If you type a nonexistent range name, 1-2-3 for Windows displays an error message. Press Esc or Enter or choose OK to clear the error. Then try again.

To name a range

1 Select the cell or range you want to name.

2 Choose **R**ange **N**ame. The Name dialog box appears.

> **Shortcut**
>
> Click the Create/Delete Range Name SmartIcon.

3 Type the new range name.

4 Choose **A**dd to create the new range name.

5 Choose OK.

You also can choose the range after selecting the **R**ange **N**ame command. Choose the command, then click the range selector in the **R**ange text box to highlight a new range.

You can type or refer to the name by using any combination of uppercase and lowercase letters, but 1-2-3 for Windows stores all range names as uppercase letters. Note the following rules and precautions for naming ranges:

- Don't use spaces, commas, semicolons, or the following characters:

    + - * / & > < @ #

- You can use numbers in range names, but don't start the name with a number.

- Don't use range names that are also cell addresses, column letters or row numbers (such as A2, IV, or 100), names of keys (such as GoTo), function names (such as @SUM), or macro commands (such as FORM).

To create a range name from a label

You also can use the **R**ange **N**ame command to create range names from labels already typed into the worksheet.

By choosing the **U**se Labels button in the Name dialog box, you can automatically create range names using column and/or row labels in the highlighted range. Just specify with the **F**or Cells drop-down list whether the cells to be identified appear Above, Below, To the Right, or To the Left of the labels.

Using labels assigns range names only to cells with labels in the specified position. If you specify a range containing blank cells, the blank cells are ignored. If you specify cells that are blank, or that include numbers or formulas, 1-2-3 ignores them.

To delete an unwanted range name, choose **R**ange **N**ame and then select the name from the list of names shown. Now choose the **D**elete button. To delete all range names in a file, choose the De**l**ete All button.

Naming Worksheets

Naming worksheets with descriptive names helps you locate the worksheet you want to use. Instead of using the default worksheet names, such as A, B, C, and so forth, on the worksheet tabs, you can assign names using a maximum of 15 characters. These names can be used in place of sheet letters in any formula, @function, or macro.

You can type a name by using any combination of uppercase and lowercase letters. Note the following rules and precautions for naming worksheets:

- Don't use spaces, commas, semicolons, or the following characters:

    + - * / & > < @ #

- You can use numbers in worksheet names, but don't start the name with a number.

- Don't use range names that are also cell addresses, column letters or row numbers (such as A2, IV, or 100), names of keys (such as GoTo), function names (such as @SUM), or macro commands (such as FORM).

To name a worksheet

1 Double-click the worksheet tab.

2 Type the name.

3 Press Enter or click the worksheet.

To name worksheets automatically

After you have named a worksheet, you can automatically name other sheets you insert next to the named sheet. 1-2-3 recognizes the same sequences for naming worksheets as the ones for filling ranges by example. (See *Filling Ranges*.)

For example, if you name a worksheet Expenses94, sheets you insert after this worksheet are automatically named Expenses95, Expenses96, and so on. If you insert two sheets before Expenses94, they are automatically named Expenses93 and Expenses92. The numeric portion of these names is recognized by 1-2-3 as part of a fill sequence. You can name a worksheet automatically only if 1-2-3 recognizes the name, or part of the name, as a fill sequence.

1 Name a worksheet that is to be the basis for automatically naming other sheets. Click the tab to select the sheet.

2 Choose **E**dit **I**nsert. The Insert dialog box appears.

> **Shortcut**
>
> To insert a sheet *after* the active sheet, click the New Sheet button
>
> or
>
> Click the Insert Sheet SmartIcon.

3 Select the **S**heet option button.

4 Select the **B**efore or A**f**ter option button, and specify the number of sheets to insert in the **Q**uantity spin box.

5 Choose OK. The sheets are inserted, automatically named.

To delete a worksheet name

1 Double-click the tab of the worksheet name you want to delete. The worksheet tab is highlighted.

2 Press Del or the Backspace key. The worksheet name is cleared from the tab.

3 Press Enter. The worksheet name is deleted, and changes to a default letter.

Navigating the Worksheet

Moving around in the worksheet is one of the key tasks you must learn to use 1-2-3 for Windows effectively.

Using the Navigator

At the left end of the edit line of the control panel is a box called the *selection indicator*. The selection indicator shows the cell address or range address currently selected in the worksheet. If the selection is a named range, only the range name is shown in the selection indicator box.

The icon to the right of the selection indicator is the *Navigator*. The Navigator is useful only if you have named ranges in the worksheet. (See *Naming Ranges*.) When you click the Navigator, a drop-down list of existing range names is displayed. Click on a range name in the list and 1-2-3 highlights that range of the worksheet.

The Navigator can also be used to supply range names while entering a formula. Begin the formula or function—for example, type **@SUM(**. Click the Navigator to display the drop-down list of range names. Click a range name—for example, SALES. Complete the formula, clicking other range names as appropriate. Press Enter to complete the formula. In this example, the cell displays @SUM(SALES).

Using the 3D Worksheet Tabs

Every time you insert another sheet into a 1-2-3 worksheet, a new tab is added to the top edge of the worksheet. Visually, the screen appears to have a stack of worksheet folders, each with its own tab. You can create up to 256 tabbed sheets in a 1-2-3 file. If you create more worksheet tabs than can be displayed on-screen, use the scroll buttons to the left of the New Sheet button to view the other tabs. You can easily navigate through the sheets of the worksheet by clicking the tabs, especially if you name the tabs according to the contents of each sheet. (See *Naming Worksheets*.) Keep in mind that the longer the sheet name, the wider the tab, allowing fewer tabs to be visible on a single screen of the worksheet.

You can also emphasize sheet tabs by changing the color of any tab. Choose the **S**tyle **W**orksheet Defaults command. Select a color from the Wor**k**sheet tab drop-down color palette, and then click OK.

Using the Keyboard

Most keys in the alphanumeric section match the keys of typewriters, and most maintain their usual functions in 1-2-3 for Windows. Several keys, however, have new and unique purposes or are not included on typewriter keyboards.

You use the keys in the numeric keypad (on the right side of the keyboard) to enter numbers or to move the cell pointer or cursor around the screen.

The function keys produce special actions. You can use these keys to access 1-2-3 for Windows editing functions, for example, or to calculate a worksheet or call up Help information. These keys are located across the top of the enhanced keyboard and on the left side of some keyboards.

The special keys include Del (Delete), Ins (Insert), Esc (Escape), Num Lock, Scroll Lock, Break, Print Screen, and Pause. These keys, which control special actions, are located in different places on different keyboards. You use some of these keys alone or with Alt, Ctrl, or Shift to perform additional actions.

Only the enhanced keyboard has a separate section for the direction keys: Home, End, PgUp, PgDn, and the four arrow keys (up, down, left, and right). On the enhanced keyboard, you can use the numeric keypad to enter numbers and the separate direction keys to move around the worksheet.

The following sections list the 1-2-3 for Windows special functions provided by the different key sections.

1-2-3 for Windows Keys

You can use specific keys on the keyboard to perform special 1-2-3 operations. The following sections define the various keys and describe the operations for which they are used.

The accelerator keys

The accelerator keys provide shortcut methods of executing common Windows and 1-2-3 for Windows commands.

Key(s)	Action(s)
Alt+Backspace *or* Ctrl+Z	Same as **E**dit **U**ndo; reverses the effect of the last command or action that can be undone
Alt+F4	Same as **F**ile E**x**it; ends the 1-2-3 session, prompts you to save any unsaved files, and returns you to Program Manager

Key(s)	Action(s)
Ctrl+Esc	Displays the Task List, which enables you to switch from one application to another
Ctrl+F4	Same as **F**ile **C**lose; closes the current window and prompts you to save the file if it contains unsaved changes
Ctrl+F6	Same as choosing Nex**t** from the Control menu of a Worksheet window; in 1-2-3 for Windows, makes the next open worksheet, graph, or transcript window active
Ctrl+Ins *or* Ctrl+C	Same as **E**dit **C**opy; copies selected data and related formatting from the worksheet to the Clipboard
Ctrl+O	Same as **F**ile **O**pen; displays the Open File dialog box, in which you can specify a file to view on-screen
Ctrl+P	Same as **F**ile **P**rint; displays the Print dialog box, which contains options for printing the current file
Ctrl+S	Same as **F**ile **S**ave; saves the current file on disk under its current name
Ctrl+Gray +	Same as **E**dit **I**nsert; inserts cells, rows, columns, or sheets (depending on your selection) into the active worksheet (use + on numeric keypad)
Ctrl+Gray −	Same as **E**dit **D**elete; removes cells, rows, columns, or sheets (depending on your selection) from the active worksheet (use − on numeric keypad)
Ctrl+*letter*	Same as **T**ools **M**acro **R**un; executes a macro in 1-2-3 for Windows
Del	Same as **E**dit Cl**e**ar; deletes selected data and related formatting without moving it to the Clipboard
Shift+Del *or* Ctrl+X	Same as **E**dit Cu**t**; moves selected data and related formatting fromthe worksheet to the Clipboard
Shift+Ins *or* Ctrl+V	Same as **E**dit **P**aste; copies selected data and related formatting from the Clipboard to the worksheet

The editing keys

You use the *editing keys* to make changes in a cell or in a dialog box.

Key(s)	Action(s)
← *or* →	Moves the cursor one character to the right or left
↑ *or* ↓	Completes the entry and moves the cell pointer up or down one cell if the entry is only one line in the control panel; if the entry is more than one line in the control panel, moves the cursor up or down one line
Backspace	Erases the character to the left of the cursor
Ctrl+←	Moves the cursor to the beginning of the preceding word
Ctrl+→	Moves the cursor to the beginning of the following word
Ctrl+PgUp *or* Ctrl+PgDn	Completes editing; in multiple worksheets, moves the cell pointer forward or back one worksheet
Del	Erases the character to the right of the cursor or erases the highlighted selection
End	Moves the cursor to after the last character in the entry
Enter	Completes editing of a cell. Pastes data and styles from the Clipboard to the worksheet when selected immediately after cutting or copying
Esc	Erases all characters in the entry
F2 (Edit)	Switches 1-2-3 between Edit mode and Ready, Value, or Label mode
F9 (Calc)	Converts a formula to its current value (if 1-2-3 is in Edit or Value mode)
Home	Moves the cursor before the first character in the entry
PgUp *or* PgDn	Completes editing and moves the cell pointer up or down one worksheet screen

Navigating the Worksheet

The file-navigation keys
You use the *file-navigation keys* to move among open files.

Key(s)	Action(s)
Ctrl+End Home	Moves to the cell last highlighted in the first open file
Ctrl+End End	Moves to the cell last highlighted in the last open file
Ctrl+End Ctrl+PgUp	Moves to the cell last highlighted in the next open file
Ctrl+End Ctrl+PgDn	Moves to the cell last highlighted in the preceding open file
Ctrl+F6	Makes the next open worksheet, graph, or transcript window active

The direction keys
The *direction keys* move the cell pointer around the worksheet when 1-2-3 is in Ready mode. In Point mode, these keys move the cell pointer and specify a range in the worksheet.

Key(s)	Action(s)
→ or ←	Moves right or left one column
↑ or ↓	Moves up or down one row
Ctrl+←	Moves left one worksheet screen
Ctrl+→ or Tab	Moves right one worksheet screen
Ctrl+Home	Moves to cell A:A1 in the current file
Ctrl+PgUp	Moves to the following worksheet
Ctrl+PgDn	Moves to the preceding worksheet

(continues)

Key(s)	Action(s)
End+→ or End+←	Moves right or left to a cell that contains data and is next to a blank cell
End+↑ or End+↓	Moves up or down to a cell that contains data and is next to a blank cell
End Ctrl+Home	Moves to the bottom right corner of the current file's active area
End Ctrl+PgUp	Staying in the same row and column, moves back through worksheets to a cell that contains data and is next to a blank cell
End Ctrl+PgDn	Staying in the same row and column, moves forward through worksheets to a cell that contains data and is next to a blank cell
End Home	Moves to the bottom right corner of the worksheet's active area
Home	Moves to cell A1 in the current worksheet
PgUp or PgDn	Moves up or down one worksheet screen

The alphanumeric keys

Many of the *alphanumeric keys* perform the same actions as the corresponding keys on a typewriter. Some of these keys, however, have special meanings in 1-2-3 for Windows.

Key(s)	Action(s)
/ (slash) or < (less than)	Activates the 1-2-3 Classic menu (see *Menus*)
[:](colon)	Activates the 1-2-3 Classic Wysiwyg menu

Key(s)	Action(s)
. (period)	If used in a range address, separates the address of the cell at the beginning of the range from the address of the cell at the end of the range; in Point mode, moves the anchor cell to another corner of the range
Alt	Used alone, activates the command menu; used with the function keys, provides additional functions
Alt+Backspace	Same as **E**dit **U**ndo; cancels the last action or command you executed
Backspace	Erases the preceding character as you enter or edit data; erases a range address during prompts that suggest a range; displays the preceding Help screen if you are using the Help utility
Caps Lock	Shifts the letter keys to uppercase (unlike the shift-lock key on a typewriter, Caps Lock has no effect on numbers and symbols)
Ctrl	Used with several keys to change their functions; used with certain preassigned keys to invoke commands quickly
Enter	In a worksheet, completes editing of a cell; in a dialog box, confirms the dialog-box settings and executes the command
Shift	Used with a letter, produces an uppercase letter; used with a number or symbol, produces the shifted character on that key; used with Num Lock and the numeric keypad, produces a direction key

The style keys

The *style keys* change the styles applied to a range of data.

Key(s)	Action(s)
Ctrl+B	Adds or removes boldface
Ctrl+I	Adds or removes italic
Ctrl+U	Adds or removes underlining
Ctrl+N	Removes bold, italic, and underlining
Ctrl+L	Left-aligns data in each cell
Ctrl+R	Right-aligns data in each cell
Ctrl+E	Centers data in each cell

The function keys

You use the 10 *function keys*—F1 through F10—to perform special actions in 1-2-3 for Windows. You can use the function keys alone or with the Alt, Shift, and Ctrl keys for additional features.

Key(s)	Action(s)
F1 (Help)	Displays a Help topic
F2 (Edit)	Places 1-2-3 in Edit mode so that you can edit an entry
F3 (Name)	Lists names of files, graphs, ranges, functions, and macro commands
F4 (Abs)	In Point or Value mode, changes the cell references in formulas from relative to absolute to mixed and back to relative; in Ready mode, anchors the cell pointer so that you can select a range
F5 (GoTo)	Same as **E**dit **G**o To; moves the cell pointer to a cell, worksheet, or active file

Key(s)	Action(s)
F6 (Pane)	Moves the cell pointer between panes
F7 (Query)	Updates the data in a query table
F8 (Table)	Repeats the last **R**ange **A**nalyze **W**hat-if Table command
F9 (Calc)	In Ready mode, recalculates formulas; in Edit or Value mode, converts a formula to its current value
F10 (Menu)	Activates the 1-2-3 menu bar; same as Alt
Alt+F1 (Compose)	Creates characters in 1-2-3 that you cannot enter directly from your keyboard
Alt+F2 (Step)	Turns Step mode on or off
Alt+F3 (Run)	Selects a macro to run
Alt+F6 (Zoom)	Enlarges the current horizontal, vertical, or perspective pane to the full size of the window or shrinks the pane to its original size
Alt+F7 (Add-In 1) *or* Alt+F8 (Add-In 2) *or* Alt+F9 (Add-In 3)	Starts a 1-2-3 add-in assigned to the key

Using the Mouse

As does the keyboard, the mouse enables you to select commands and manipulate objects on-screen. You can perform many tasks more quickly by using the mouse. Some tasks in 1-2-3 can be performed *only* by using a mouse. As you perform different tasks in 1-2-3 for Windows, the mouse pointer changes shape.

Most mouse devices have a left and a right button. You use the left button to select cells and ranges, use menus, and enter information in dialog boxes. You use the right button to access additional features, such as quick menus or SmartIcon descriptions.

The following table describes the mouse terminology you need to know as you read this book.

Term	Meaning
Click	Press and quickly release the left mouse button
Double-click	Quickly press and release the left mouse button twice
Click and drag	Press and hold the left mouse button and then move the mouse. This moves the mouse pointer, usually to highlight a range or after grabbing an object
Grab	Move the mouse pointer to the object to be moved and press and hold the left mouse button. You then can drag the object. The mouse pointer looks like a closed (grabbing) hand while you drag the object
Point	Place the mouse pointer over the menu, cell, or data you want to select or move

Notes

1-2-3 Release 5 for Windows enables you to exchange data between 1-2-3 and Lotus Notes Release 3.0 or later by embedding a 1-2-3 worksheet in a Notes form. Users can create spreadsheets using the same 1-2-3 template, then store the spreadsheets in a Notes database. When you open a Notes form containing an embedded worksheet, Notes starts 1-2-3 to allow you to enter data into the worksheet. The information is shared with Notes and is stored in a Notes database.

With the 1-2-3 Version Manager, several Lotus Notes users can work on the same spreadsheet file concurrently. 1-2-3 creates separate range versions, locking the ranges currently in use to avoid the problem of overwriting each others' data. Notes provides access control to determine who is allowed to add or modify various contributions to the worksheet.

Even though the data is stored as a Notes database, you can open the file in 1-2-3 and do not need to work with the Notes interface. If another concurrent user posts changes to the file during your 1-2-3 session, 1-2-3 will beep and display the message New versions have been posted in the title bar. Open the Notes database to display a view similar to the Version Manager Index view in 1-2-3. All versions can be monitored to control modifications to the worksheet.

Number Formatting

The first option on the 1-2-3 for Windows **S**tyle menu is **N**umber Format. You use this option to assign a specific number format to a cell or range of cells. Assigning a format to cells maintains consistency throughout the worksheet and saves you the effort of typing symbols (dollar signs, commas, parentheses, and so on) along with the cell value.

Number formats apply only to numeric data (numeric formulas and numbers). If you format a label as Fixed or Scientific, for example, the number format has no effect on how a label appears. One exception to this rule is the Hidden format, which can apply to both labels and string formulas.

The following table shows samples of the available cell formats and how each one changes the appearance of data. Date formats in this table assume that the current year is 1994.

Number Formatting

Format	Entry	Displayed
General	**1234**	1234
General	**1234.5**	1234.5
Fixed, 2 decimal places	**1234.5**	1234.50
Fixed, 0 decimal places	**1234.5**	1235
, Comma, 2 decimal places	**1234.5**	1,234.50
US Dollar, 2 decimal places	**1234.5**	$1,234.50
British Pound, 2 decimal places	**1234.5**	£1,234.50
Canadian Dollar, 2 decimal places	**1234.5**	C$1,234.50
Japanese Yen, 0 decimal places	**1234**	¥1,234
Mexican Peso, 2 decimal places	**1234.5**	Mex$1,234.50
Percent, 1 decimal place	**0.364**	36.4%
Scientific, 4 decimal places	**1234.5**	1.2345E+03
+/−	**5**	+++++
31-Dec-93 (date format)	**2/14/94**	14-Feb-94
31-Dec (date format)	**2/14/94**	14-Feb
Dec-93 (date format)	**2/14/94**	Feb-94
12/31/93 (date format)	**2/14/94**	02/14/94
12/31 (date format)	**2/14/94**	02/14
11:59:59 AM (time format)	**10:15**	10:15:00 AM
11:59 AM (time format)	**10:15**	10:15 AM
23:59:59 (time format)	**10:15**	10:15:00
23:59 (time format)	**10:15**	10:15
Text	**+C6**	+C6

Format	Entry	Displayed
Hidden	**1234.5**	No display
Label	**57 Main St.**	57 Main St.
Automatic	**1234.5**	1234.5

If a column isn't wide enough to display a formatted numeric entry, asterisks fill the cell. If the numeric entry is unformatted and too long to fit in the cell, 1-2-3 for Windows converts the entry to scientific notation. To display the data, you must change the format or the column width.

To assign number formats

1 To change the format of a cell or range, choose **S**tyle **N**umber Format. The Number Format dialog box appears.

If you preselected a range, that range is listed in the R**a**nge text box; if you did not preselect a range, specify one in the dialog box.

2 Select one of the formats from the **F**ormat list box. You can select a format by typing the initial character of the format (such as **F** for Fixed) or by using the arrow keys or the mouse.

3 If you choose Fixed, Scientific, , Comma, Currency, or Percent, you can specify the number of decimal places or use the default number, 2, shown in the **D**ecimal Places box.

To change the number of decimal places, type another number between 0 and 15 or use the scroll arrows to change the number. For some formats like General, the **D**ecimal Places text box doesn't appear in the dialog box.

4 If you choose Currency in the **F**ormat list box, you can select from over 40 currency types or use the default, US Dollar, shown in the **C**urrency list box.

Note the appearance of the selected currency type in the Sample box. If you want to specify a currency type other than the ones listed, select Other Country, and then choose the **M**odify Symbol button to display the Modify Symbol dialog box. Type a symbol in the **S**ymbol text box, then select whether to position the symbol **B**efore or **A**fter the value. (You can also modify the symbol for any of the existing currency types in the Currency list box.) Choose OK to return to the Number Format dialog box.

If you have chosen a currency type that does not already show in the format selector in the status bar, select the **S**how in Status Bar check box to make the currency type available in the format selector.

5 If you choose Dates or Times in the **F**ormat list box, the Dat**e**s list box or **T**imes list box is displayed. Select a format from the list.

6 If you want to enclose all values in the select range in parentheses, select the **P**arens check box.

7 Click OK to close the Number Format dialog box and change the format of the selected range.

> **Tip**
>
> Click the following SmartIcons to apply common number formats to values in a selected range:
>
> | 0,0 | Default thousands separator and no decimal places |
> | % | Value as a percentage, percent sign and two decimal places |
> | $ | US Dollar currency symbol, the default thousands separator, and two decimal places |
> | £ | British Pound currency symbol, the default thousands separator, and two decimal places. |
> | ¥ | Japanese Yen currency symbol, the default thousands separator, and no decimal places. |

You can use the **R**eset button in the Number Format dialog box to quickly restore the default number format (that is, the format specified in the Worksheet Defaults dialog box) to the selected cell or range.

The format selector in the status bar displays the format of the current cell. For example, Fixed appears on the format selector when the current cell is formatted with the Fixed format. The number of decimal places for the current cell appears on the decimal selector.

> **Tip**
>
> Click the format selector to quickly change the format of a range. Click the decimal selector to quickly change the number of decimal places displayed for numbers in the range.

To set number format defaults

1 Choose **S**tyle **W**orksheet Defaults. The Worksheet Defaults dialog box appears.

2 In the Number Format area, select a format from the F**o**rmat drop-down list.

Based on the format chosen, other boxes may appear. Make a selection as described in the steps in the previous section.

3 Choose the Display **Z**eros As check box if you want to change the display of zero values or formulas resulting in zero. For example, instead of a 0 character, you can display nothing (a blank cell) or a label such as ZERO.

4 To display all new values in parentheses, choose the **P**arentheses check box.

5 Choose OK to set the new defaults for the current worksheet.

Opening Files

When you choose the **F**ile **O**pen command, 1-2-3 displays the file you open in the current window. Other open worksheet files remain open. All open files are listed on the **W**indow menu.

To open a file

1 Choose **F**ile **O**pen. The Open File dialog box appears.

> **Shortcut**
>
> Click the Open File SmartIcon.

2 The current directory name appears above the **D**irectories box. Files in the current directory are listed in the files list box. In the File **N**ame text box, type the name of the file you want to open. Alternatively, you can select the file from the files list box.

To open files from subdirectories and other drives

If the file you want to open is located in a different directory, select the directory from the **D**irectories list box. If necessary, use the scroll bar or arrow keys to display all entries in the file list or **D**irectories box. After you choose a directory, choose a file to open, and then click OK.

If the file you want to open is stored on another drive, select the appropriate drive in the **D**rives drop-down box. When you select a different drive, 1-2-3 displays all files on that drive in the files list. Select a file from the files list, and then choose OK.

To open multiple files at once

If you plan to use more than one worksheet from the same directory, you can open them at the same time, rather than repeatedly choosing File Open. Select the first file, then hold down the Ctrl key while selecting other files. If the files you want to open are listed consecutively, click on the first file, then drag to include all the files you want to open. You can have up to 32 files open at the same time; however, this is probably not practical. Also, you may not have enough system memory to handle that many open files.

To use wild cards to open files

In the Open File dialog box, you can include an asterisk (*) or a question mark (?) as *wild cards* in the File **N**ame box. Wild cards act as placeholders that match one character or any number of characters in sequence. The ? wild card matches any one character in the file name. The * matches any number of characters in sequence. When you use wild cards in a File **N**ame text box, 1-2-3 for Windows lists only the files whose names match the wild card.

The *.wk* in the File **N**ame box tells 1-2-3 to list all files with file extensions that begin with .WK followed by any number of other characters. If you type **BUDGET*.*** in the File **N**ame text box, 1-2-3 for Windows lists all the file names that start with BUDGET, such as BUDGET.WK4, BUDGET1.TXT, and BUDGET99.WK3.

To open a file automatically when you start 1-2-3

When you first start 1-2-3 for Windows, a blank worksheet appears so that you can create a new file. However, if you usually begin a work session using the same worksheet file, you can tell 1-2-3 to automatically display that worksheet when the program starts. You do this by naming the file AUTO123.WK4.

Another way to open a specific worksheet in 1-2-3 is to use the Windows File Manager. Without starting 1-2-3, open the File Manager. In the File Manager window, select the 123R5W directory (or a subdirectory where the file is located) to display all the files in the directory. Double-click on the name of the file you want to open. Because worksheet files have a WK4 file extension, the file you select is associated with the 1-2-3 for Windows program. The Windows File Manager knows to open the 1-2-3 for Windows program as well as the file you select.

To open recently used files

1-2-3 provides a convenient feature that enables you to quickly open the files you used most recently. This feature saves you the trouble of selecting a file name from the Open File dialog box when you want to open a file. To list on the File menu the most recently used files, choose the Tools User Setup command. In the User Setup dialog box, enter a number between 0 and 5 in the Number of Recent Files To Show box, and then click OK. 1-2-3 adds the names of the files (up to the number you specify) at the bottom of the File menu. To open a file, simply click the file name on the File menu.

To open spreadsheet files from other programs

1-2-3 Release 5 for Windows enables you to open text files and files from previous releases of 1-2-3, SmartMasters, Lotus Notes, Symphony, dBASE, Paradox, and Excel. The following table lists these programs and their file extensions.

Extension	Program
DB	Paradox files
DBF	dBASE files
NS4	Shared files using Lotus Notes
TXT, CSV, PRN	Text files created by any program (other extensions possible)
WK3, FM3	1-2-3 for Windows Release 1; 1-2-3 for DOS Release 3
WKS	1-2-3 for DOS Release 1A
WK1, ALL, FMT	1-2-3 for DOS Release 2
WRK	Symphony Releases 1.0 and 1.01
WR1, FMS	Symphony Releases 1.1, 1.2, 2.0, 2.1, 2.2, and 3.0
WT4	SmartMaster template files created in 1-2-3 Release 5
XLS	Microsoft Excel Versions 2.1, 3.0, and 4.0

To open any of these files, select the file type in the File **T**ype drop-down list in the Open File dialog box. Select the file from the correct directory, and then click OK. You can save these files in their original file formats, or you can save them as 1-2-3 Release 5 (WK4) files. Keep in mind, however, that if you add features to the file that are available only in 1-2-3 Release 5, these features are lost when you save the file in its original file format.

Outlines

See *Borders*

Passwords

See *Protecting Files and Data*

Previewing Data

You can find and fix many minor errors before printing if you use the 1-2-3 Print Preview feature. With Print Preview, you can see how 1-2-3 for Windows breaks up a large print range over several pages, how multiple ranges fit on one or more pages, whether the specified margins are appropriate, and so on.

To preview a print job, you can use any of the following methods:

- Choose the **F**ile Print Pre**v**iew command.
- Choose the **F**ile **P**rint command. From the resulting Print dialog box, choose the **P**review button.

> **Shortcut**
>
> Click the Preview SmartIcon. This SmartIcon is available in the default palette as well as the Printing palette.

All these methods access the Print Preview dialog box. Use the Print Preview dialog box to specify whether you want to preview the Current **W**orksheet, **A**ll Worksheets, a Selected **R**ange, or a range of pages. Before accessing this dialog box, you can preselect a print range to automatically enter it into the Selected **R**ange field in the dialog box.

After you finish specifying the options in the Print Preview dialog box, choose OK or press Enter to preview the worksheet. 1-2-3 for Windows displays the preview in a special preview window. Notice that the menu options are inactive and that the SmartIcon palette changes. Position the mouse pointer over each SmartIcon to view its description in the title bar.

Preview the current page, or select the appropriate SmartIcon to view two facing pages or several pages at once. You can also scroll through the data in the Preview window using the scroll bars. Click the left mouse button on the preview page to toggle through the zoom magnifications. If you are satisfied with the appearance of the print preview, click the Print SmartIcon to display the Print dialog box. Or, to return to the worksheet, click the rightmost SmartIcon, which closes the Print Preview window.

Printing Data

With 1-2-3 for Windows, you are always in a Wysiwyg (what-you-see-is-what-you-get) environment—what you see on-screen closely resembles the printed output on paper. Some obvious differences can occur. For example, many users have color monitors but print on black-and-white printers. In this case, 1-2-3 for Windows enables you to select different shades of gray or patterns to represent different colors when you print graphs.

To use the default print settings

In 1-2-3 for Windows, you use the File Printer Setup commands to set printer defaults. Because you are using Windows, many printer settings are already in place. The Windows environment retains basic information about the printer, even when you use 1-2-3 for Windows.

By using the Windows control panel in the Main program group of the Program Manager, you can change the hardware-specific printer defaults. You can add or delete printer drivers and set other printer defaults (such as the kind of paper feed, orientation, and paper size). Refer to the Windows documentation for details on changing these defaults.

To set up the printer

The primary use of the File Printer Setup command is to select the printer to which you want to send the report if you have more than one printer. You also can use Printer Setup to specify additional print settings such as the orientation of the print job on the paper (portrait or landscape), scaling, paper size, paper source, and number of copies. You set these options by clicking the Setup button in the Printer Setup dialog box. This dialog box has additional settings you can change by clicking on its Options button. The exact options available depend on the printer you select.

To set up the page

You select most printing options through the Page Setup dialog box, accessed by choosing Page Setup from the File menu. You also can access this dialog box from the Print and Print Preview dialog boxes (displayed by selecting the File Print and File Print Preview commands, respectively).

Shortcut
Click the Page Setup SmartIcon.

The Page Setup dialog box includes options for specifying orientation, margins, header and footer information, size, frame, grid lines, and print titles. You also can assign a name to a particular group of settings and later use these settings from any worksheet. You can designate the current settings as the default settings, or you can restore the default settings to replace the current settings.

To specify the print range

Before you can print anything, you have to tell 1-2-3 what you want to print. To preselect a print range, you use one of two methods:

- With the mouse, click and drag to highlight the range.

- With the keyboard, press the F4 key to anchor one corner of the range and then use the arrow keys to define the extent of the range; press Enter when finished defining the range.

If you forget to preselect the range you want to print, you can specify the range in the Selected **R**ange text box of the Print or Print Preview dialog box. You can type the cell addresses, enter a range name, or highlight the range from this text box. To highlight the print range, first click the range selector and then select the range in the normal fashion. With the mouse, use the click-and-drag or shift-click technique. With the keyboard, use Backspace to unanchor any previously selected range, position the cell pointer at the start of the desired range, press the period key to anchor the range, and then use the direction keys (Home, End, PgUp, PgDn, and the arrow keys) to designate the print range.

To insert manual page breaks

If you are unhappy with the way 1-2-3 splits the data in a long report, you can insert manual page breaks—both horizontal and vertical varieties. A horizontal page break controls a long worksheet; a vertical page break controls a wide worksheet. To insert a page break, move the cell pointer to where you want the page break to occur. Horizontal breaks are inserted *above* the cell pointer; vertical breaks are inserted to the *left* of the cell pointer. When you insert manual page breaks, you see dotted lines that represent the placement of these breaks.

To insert a page break, follow these steps:

1 Place the cell pointer in the first row below where you want the break to occur, or in the first column to the right of where you want the break to occur.

2 Choose **S**tyle Page **B**reak.

> **Shortcut**
>
>   Click the Horizontal Page Break or Vertical Page Break SmartIcon.

3 If you use the SmartIcon, 1-2-3 immediately displays a dotted line indicating the page break in the worksheet. The **S**tyle Page **B**reak command, on the other hand, displays the Page Break dialog box, from which you can choose **C**olumn (for a vertical page break) or **R**ow (for a horizontal page break).

4 After specifying the type of page break you want in the Page Break dialog box, click OK or press Enter. A dotted line indicating the page break appears in the worksheet.

To remove page breaks, choose **S**tyle Page **B**reak and uncheck the **C**olumn or **R**ow box.

To print data

Choose the **F**ile **P**rint command to start the printing process.

> **Shortcut**
>
> Press Ctrl+P.
>
> or
>
> Click the Print SmartIcon.

When you choose **F**ile **P**rint, 1-2-3 for Windows displays the Print dialog box. Use this dialog box to specify the pages you want to print, the number of copies you need, the range or ranges to print, and so on. The Page **S**etup button accesses the Page Setup dialog box (described in the preceding section). When you close the Page Setup dialog box, you return to the Print dialog box. The **P**review button displays a preview of the printed output. When you finish looking at the preview, you return to the worksheet.

To switch the page orientation

One way to get a wide report to fit on a single page is to change the *orientation* (direction) of the printing. Normally you print in *portrait orientation*; that is, the text prints vertically on the page, with the top of the printout at the narrow edge of the paper. If you print horizontally on the page, you use *landscape orientation*.

You can change the orientation in the Page Setup dialog box (choose **F**ile Pa**g**e Setup). Choose **P**ortrait or Lan**d**scape to indicate the direction you want 1-2-3 to print.

Shortcut
Click the Portrait or Landscape SmartIcon.

The SmartIcons and the Page Setup dialog box change the orientation for the current file only. If you want to change the setting permanently for your printer, choose **F**ile Prin**t**er Setup, select the printer you want to change, choose **S**etup, and then specify the orientation for the printer in the resulting dialog box.

To compress or expand the report

If your report doesn't fit on one page, you can have 1-2-3 automatically shrink the data using the Si**z**e option in the Page Setup dialog box. Five sizes are available:

- Actual Size
- Fit All to Page

- Fit Columns to Page
- Fit Rows to Page
- Manually Scale

With Actual Size (the default setting), the data is not compressed at all. If you select Fit All to Page, 1-2-3 compresses the print range in an attempt to fit all the information on one page. If the print range still does not fit, 1-2-3 prints the first page with the most compression possible and subsequent pages with the same compression. Or choose to compress just the columns (Fit Columns to Page) or just the rows (Fit Rows to Page).

You also may enter a specific percentage by choosing the Manually Scale option. If you select this option, the dialog box displays a text box in which you can enter a percentage; this number can be as low as 15 (representing 15 percent of normal size) or as high as 1000 (representing 1000 percent, or 10 times the normal size). By manually scaling, you can compress or expand the worksheet.

> **Shortcut**
>
>   The Printing SmartIcon palette offers three SmartIcons for fitting the print range on a single page: Fit Rows to Page, Fit Columns to Page, and Fit All to Page.

To create headers and footers

1-2-3 for Windows reserves three lines at the top of each page for a header and an additional three lines at the bottom for a footer. These lines are reserved whether or not you enter header and footer text. The header text, which is printed on the first line after the top margin, is followed by two blank header lines preceding the report (for spacing). The footer text is printed above the bottom margin and below two blank footer lines (again, for spacing).

You specify a header or footer in the Page Setup dialog box. A header or footer can have three parts; boxes are provided for each part in the Page Setup dialog box. Whatever you enter in the first box is aligned at the left margin; the text in the second box is centered between the left and right margins; the text in the third box is aligned at the right margin.

In addition to any text you enter, the header or footer can include codes for inserting page numbers, the date or time of printing, the file name, or the contents of a cell. First, place the cursor in the appropriate box (left-aligned, centered, or right-aligned) next to **H**eader or **F**ooter in the Page Setup dialog box. The insert icons immediately become active. Then specify the codes you want to use from the following list:

- To number pages sequentially (starting with 1), enter a pound sign (#) or click the page-number insert icon (the center icon).

- To print the current date, enter an at sign (@) or click the date insert icon (the calendar).

- To print the time, enter a plus sign (+) or click the time insert icon (the clock).

- To insert the file name, type a caret symbol (^) or click the file-name insert icon (the one that looks like a page).

- To use the contents of a cell as a header or footer, enter a backslash (\) or click the cell-contents insert icon (it looks like a worksheet grid). Then type the address or range name of the cell that contains the text you want to include in the header or footer. The specified cell address or range name can contain a formula. If you specify a range name, 1-2-3 for Windows uses the contents of only the first cell in the range.

See also *Headers and Footers*

To print titles

To make a multiple-page printed report more understandable, you can add headings from row or column ranges by using the Print Titles options in the Page Setup dialog box. Setting titles in a printout is similar to freezing titles in the worksheet. To specify row titles in the Ro**w**s box of the Page Setup dialog box, select one or more rows of labels to print above each print range and at the top of all pages. To specify column titles in the **C**olumns box of the Page Setup dialog box, designate one or more columns of labels to print to the left of every print range and at the left edge of all pages.

> **Shortcut**
>
> 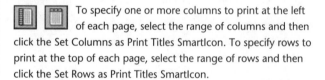 To specify one or more columns to print at the left of each page, select the range of columns and then click the Set Columns as Print Titles SmartIcon. To specify rows to print at the top of each page, select the range of rows and then click the Set Rows as Print Titles SmartIcon.

If you include the print titles in the print range, 1-2-3 prints these elements twice. Be careful, therefore, not to include the range containing the print titles in the print range.

To cancel a print title, highlight the entry in the **C**olumns or Ro**w**s text box in the Page Setup dialog box. Press Del to clear the contents and then press Enter.

To print the worksheet frame and grid lines

Printing the worksheet frame is particularly useful during worksheet development, when you want the printouts to show the location of data in a large worksheet. In the Show section of the Page Setup dialog box, you can make two selections to print the worksheet frame. The Wor**k**sheet Frame option prints column letters across the top of a worksheet and row numbers down the side of the worksheet. The **G**rid Lines option prints lines between all cells in the print range.

To set margins
The Page Setup dialog box enables you to change the margins of the report. Select **T**op, **B**ottom, **L**eft, or **R**ight, and enter the margin width in inches. See also *Margins*.

To center printing on page
New in Release 5, 1-2-3 for Windows enables you to print a selected range centered vertically, horizontally, or both. In the Center area of the Page Setup dialog box, choose the Horizo**n**tally check box to center the printed range between the left and right margins. Choose the Verti**ca**lly check box to center the printed range between the top and bottom margins. Choose both check boxes to center both vertically and horizontally.

Shortcut

     The Printing SmartIcon palette offers three SmartIcons for centering the printed page: Center Vertically, Center Horizontally, and Center All (to center both vertically and horizontally).

To name and save the current print settings
When you have several worksheet reports with a similar layout, you may want to save the page setup so that you can retrieve the settings for other files. Saving the page setup options keeps you from having to specify the same settings over and over again. The Named Settings area in the Page Setup dialog box offers buttons for saving and retrieving page settings.

To assign a name to the current print settings, select the **S**ave button; you are prompted for a file name. The **S**ave button creates a file, with the AL3 extension, that you can use with other worksheets. When you want to use these named settings in another worksheet file, select the Retrie**v**e button from the Page Setup dialog box and then select the file name from the list of settings file names.

To print a text file to disk
To create an ASCII text file that you can incorporate into a word processing document, you use no printing-related commands. This represents a deviation from DOS versions of 1-2-3, which use the /**P**rint **F**ile command to print a file to disk. In 1-2-3 for Windows, you create an ASCII file by selecting the **F**ile Save **A**s command and choosing the Text (txt) file type in the Save As dialog box. Enter a name in the File **N**ame field; if you don't type an extension, TXT is assigned automatically.

To stop and suspend printing
You can halt the current print job, clear the print queue, and temporarily suspend printing by accessing the Print Manager (press Ctrl+Esc and select Print Manager). To cancel the printing of a report, click the name of the file in the print queue and then click the Delete button. See the Windows manual for more information on the Print Manager.

Protecting Files and Data

1-2-3 for Windows enables you to protect data from accidental or deliberate change, as well as hide confidential data. 1-2-3 for Windows also provides features that enable others to use the file without seeing certain areas of it.

You also can password-protect a file that contains confidential data when you save the file. Anyone who does not know the password is then denied access to the file. No matter how well a person knows 1-2-3 for Windows, that person cannot access the file without the password.

The following sections describe 1-2-3 for Windows' data-protection features.

To assign passwords
When you save a file with a password, no one can open, copy, or print the file without first issuing the password. To assign a password to a file by using the **F**ile Save **A**s dialog box, follow these steps:

1. Choose **F**ile Save **A**s. The Save As dialog box appears.

2. Type the file name in the File **N**ame text box.

3. Select the **W**ith Password check box, and then click OK. The Set Password dialog box appears.

4. In the **P**assword text box, type a password.

5. In the **V**erify text box, type the password again exactly as you typed it before, and then select OK.

If you enter in the File **N**ame box a file name that already exists, 1-2-3 for Windows asks whether you want to replace the existing file, back up the existing file, or cancel saving the file. You must select **R**eplace or **B**ackup to save the file with the password. If you select Cancel, 1-2-3 for Windows doesn't assign the password and returns you to the Worksheet window.

A password can contain any combination of uppercase or lowercase characters. As you enter the password, 1-2-3 for Windows displays an asterisk for each character you type. Passwords are case-sensitive; if you specify **JustForMe** as the password, typing **justforme** to open the file does not work.

To open a password-protected file
When you try to open a password-protected file by using **F**ile **O**pen, 1-2-3 for Windows prompts you for the password. You must enter the password exactly as you originally entered it, with the correct upper- and lowercase letters. If you make an error as you enter the password, an error message appears, saying that you entered an invalid password. Try opening the file again, using the correct password.

To change and delete passwords

You can change or delete a file's password at any time, provided you know the current password. To change a password, follow the same steps you use to assign a password: choose **F**ile Save **A**s, but type a new password in the **P**assword and **V**erify text boxes.

To remove a password from a file, open the password-protected file. Choose **F**ile Save **A**s, and then turn off the **W**ith password check box. Choose OK. 1-2-3 displays a message saying that the file already exists. Choose **R**eplace or **B**ackup to save the file without a password.

To seal a file to prevent changes

Sealing a file prevents a user from changing data, styles, or other settings used in the file. When a file is sealed, you cannot insert or delete columns; show hidden worksheets or columns; change, add, or delete range names, page breaks, or frozen titles; set new formats, column widths, row heights, or cell alignments; use the style, chart, draw, or new query commands; or change the file reservation setting.

You seal a file when you want other users to be able to open and read the file, but not change it. A sealed file is also password-protected. Although you can open and read the file without knowing the password, you must know the password if you want to change the file in any way. The password protection on a sealed file allows you to give read access to a large group of users while giving only one or a few users the authority to change the file. (Without the password protection, only the user who creates the file can change it.)

To seal a file, you choose the File P**r**otect command to display the Protect dialog box. Choose the **S**eal File check box, and then click OK. 1-2-3 displays the Set Password dialog box, the same dialog box used to save a file with a password. Type the password in the **P**assword text box, and then type the password a second time in the **V**erify text box. You can use any combination of upper- and lowercase characters in the password.

To protect selected cells or a range

In some cases, you may want users to be able to change certain cells in a file, even though the file is sealed. You can leave certain cells unprotected by using the **S**tyle **P**rotection command *before* you seal the file. First, select the cells you want unprotected, and then choose **S**tyle **P**rotection to display the Protection dialog box.

The **R**ange box shows the range of cells you selected. Choose the **K**eep Data Unprotected After File Is Sealed check box, and then click OK. Now that a range of cells has been set as unprotected, you can seal the file using the steps outlined earlier. When a sealed file contains unprotected cells, the status bar displays Pr when the cell pointer is in a protected cell and U when the cell pointer is in an unprotected cell. Also, data in unprotected cells is displayed in another color.

To change protected cells in a file that has been sealed, you must unseal the file first, and then change the cell protection. To unseal a file, follow these steps:

1 Choose **F**ile **P**rotect. The Protect dialog box appears.

2 In the Protect dialog box, turn off the **S**eal File check box, and then click OK. 1-2-3 displays the Set Password dialog box.

3 Type the password in the **P**assword text box, and then click OK.

Now you can use the **S**tyle **P**rotection command to change the unprotected cells in the file.

To reserve shared files

If you use 1-2-3 for Windows on a network, two or more people can access or update the same file at the same time. If more than one person can change a file at the same time, the result can be inaccurate data or formulas. To avoid multiple updates of the same shared file, 1-2-3 for Windows has a *reservation* system. 1-2-3 for Windows also enables you to hide and protect confidential data in a shared file.

Protecting Files and Data

The **F**ile **P**rotect command displays the Protect dialog box, which enables you to **G**et or **R**elease a file reservation or change a file reservation setting to automatic or manual. By default, 1-2-3 for Windows gives you the reservation when you open a shared file. If you try to open a shared file that someone else is currently working on, 1-2-3 for Windows displays a message box that asks whether you want to open the file without having the reservation. If you select **Y**es, you can read the file and change the data, but you cannot save the changes to the same file name. You can, however, save the file with another name so that your changes are preserved.

If you have the reservation for a file, you keep the reservation until you close the file, or you can release the reservation by using **F**ile **P**rotect **R**elease. The file is still open on your computer, but you cannot save the file under the same name because you no longer have the reservation.

You can change 1-2-3 for Windows' default so that a user must get the reservation manually instead of automatically. To change the default, deselect the **F**ile **P**rotect Get Reservation **A**utomatically check box. Now, anyone who opens the file has read-only access until one user reserves the file using the **F**ile **P**rotect **G**et command.

You can seal a file's reservation setting after you change it so that no one else can change the setting. Select **F**ile **P**rotect and choose the **S**eal File option. When 1-2-3 displays the Set Password dialog box, enter a password in the **P**assword and **V**erify text boxes. Passwords are case-sensitive. Remember the password exactly as you type it. If you or someone else later tries to change the reservation setting, 1-2-3 for Windows prompts for the password.

To hide cells and ranges

Sometimes you want to do more than just stop someone from changing data or formulas; you want to prevent other users from even seeing the information. To *hide* a cell or range, follow these steps:

1 Choose **S**tyle **N**umber Format.

2 Select Hidden from the Format list. A hidden cell appears as a blank cell in the worksheet.

3 To redisplay the cell contents in the worksheet, use any other number format.

You can hide data so that it's not *easily* visible, but you cannot prevent someone from seeing hidden data if that person knows how to use 1-2-3 for Windows. The only way to keep data truly confidential is to save the file with a password.

You cannot use the Hidden format to hide data completely. If you move the cell pointer to that cell, you can see the contents of the cell in the edit line. Also, you can change the number format and view the contents in the cell again. If the file is sealed, however, you cannot change the format or view the contents of the cell in the edit line.

When you print a range containing hidden cells, columns, or worksheets, the hidden text doesn't appear in the printout.

Hidden cells *appear* empty; seal the file to prevent users from accidentally typing over the contents of hidden cells or reformatting the cells.

To hide worksheets, columns, and rows

When you hide worksheets, columns, and rows, they retain their letters and numbers, and 1-2-3 for Windows skips them in the display. If you hide columns B and C, for example, 1-2-3 for Windows displays in the column border columns A, D, E, and so on. These missing letters and numbers make the hiding of data obvious. You can make hidden data less obvious by eliminating the frame with the command View Set View Preferences and deselecting the option Worksheet Frame.

To hide a worksheet, move the cell pointer to the worksheet you want to hide, use Style Hide, and select the Sheet option in the Hide dialog box. 1-2-3 for Windows removes the worksheet from the screen, and the cell pointer moves to the next worksheet. To display a hidden worksheet, use Style Hide, type the hidden worksheet's letter in the Range text box, and click the Show button.

A hidden worksheet does not appear on-screen, but the worksheet letter is retained. Formulas that refer to cells in hidden worksheets are calculated correctly, and 1-2-3 for Windows continues to store the full value of hidden data.

To hide a column, move the cell pointer to a cell in the column you want to hide. Then use **S**tyle **H**ide and select **C**olumn. If you don't preselect one or more columns, you can type a column address in the R**a**nge text box of the Hide dialog box. To redisplay hidden columns, choose **S**tyle **H**ide and specify a range that includes cells in the hidden columns, then click Sho**w**.

When you print a range that contains hidden columns, the hidden columns do not print.

No specific command to hide a row is available, but you can use the **S**tyle **R**ow Height command to set a row's height to one, making it nearly invisible. You also can use a mouse to point to the border between the current row's number and the next row's number in the worksheet frame and then click and drag the mouse up or down to shrink or expand the height of the row. Like a hidden column, a hidden row does not appear in the worksheet, but the row number is retained. Formulas that refer to cells in hidden rows are calculated correctly, and 1-2-3 for Windows continues to store the full value of hidden data. Use the **S**tyle **R**ow Height command or the mouse to make the row visible again by changing its height to be greater than one. When you print a range that contains hidden rows, the hidden rows do not print.

Recalculating a Worksheet

When a value in a cell changes, 1-2-3 for Windows recalculates every cell that depends on the changed value. This recalculation demonstrates the power of an electronic spreadsheet. Usually, 1-2-3 recalculates a worksheet automatically when a cell changes. If you prefer, you can tell 1-2-3 for Windows that you want to recalculate manually.

Recalculating a Worksheet **189**

Unless you specify otherwise, 1-2-3 for Windows recalculates only those formulas whose values have changed since the last recalculation. If you change the data in one cell and that cell is used in one formula, 1-2-3 for Windows recalculates only that formula.

To specify the recalculation method
You can tell 1-2-3 for Windows not to recalculate the worksheet automatically by choosing **T**ools **U**ser Setup, choosing the **R**ecalculation option in the User Setup dialog box, and selecting **M**anual in the Recalculation dialog box.

Use the **T**ools **U**ser Setup **R**ecalculation command again to reset 1-2-3 for Windows to **A**utomatic recalculation.

After recalculation is set to manual, you must use one of the following methods to recalculate the worksheet:

- Press F9 (Calc).

- Click the Calc button in the status bar.

- In a macro, you can invoke recalculation with the CALC, RECALC, and RECALCON macro commands.

> **Shortcut**
>
> Click the Recalculate SmartIcon.

To specify the recalculation order
You also can control the order in which 1-2-3 for Windows recalculates. By default, 1-2-3 for Windows recalculates in **N**atural order. In *natural order recalculation*, 1-2-3 for Windows determines which formulas depend on which cells and then sets up a recalculation order to produce the correct results.

If you prefer, you can tell 1-2-3 for Windows to recalculate By **R**ow or By **C**olumn. Columnar recalculation starts in cell A1 and continues down the cells in column A, then column B, and so on. Row recalculation starts in cell A1 and continues across the cells in row 1, then row 2, and so on.

Generally, you should leave 1-2-3 for Windows set for natural order. When calculating by row or by column, 1-2-3 for Windows must sweep through columns and rows several times to make sure that formulas produce correct results. Natural order is faster because 1-2-3 for Windows first determines which cells have changed and then recalculates them in one sweep.

If you specify By **R**ow or By **C**olumn, you should tell 1-2-3 for Windows the number of *iterations* to perform (how many times to recalculate). Specify a number from 1 (the default) to 50 in the **I**terations text box. If 1-2-3 for Windows is set to recalculate in natural order and no circular references exist, 1-2-3 for Windows may stop calculating before it reaches the number of iterations indicated.

To handle circular references
The natural order of recalculation is not always accurate if a circular reference exists. A *circular reference* is a formula that depends, either directly or indirectly, on its own value. Whenever 1-2-3 for Windows performs a recalculation and finds a circular reference, the `Circ` indicator appears on the circular-reference button in the status bar. A circular reference is almost always an error, and you should correct it immediately.

If the `Circ` indicator appears and you are not sure why, click the circular-reference button on the status bar to go to the cell containing the circular reference. In this case, fixing the error is fairly easy. In other cases, the source of the problem may be less obvious, and you may have to check every cell referenced by the formula.

Regression Analysis

The **R**ange **A**nalyze **R**egression command gives you a multiple linear regression analysis package within 1-2-3 for Windows.

Use **R**ange **A**nalyze **R**egression when you want to determine the relationship between one set of values (the *dependent variable*) and one or more other sets of values (the *independent variables*). Regression analysis has a number of uses in a business setting, including relating sales to price, promotions, and other market factors; relating stock prices to earnings and interest rates; and relating production costs to production levels.

Think of linear regression as a way of determining the best line through a series of data points. Multiple regression does this for several variables simultaneously, determining the best line relating the dependent variable to the set of independent variables.

The **R**ange **A**nalyze **R**egression command can simultaneously determine how to draw a line through these data points and how well the line fits the data. When you invoke the command, the Regression dialog box appears.

Use the **X**-Range option to select one or more independent variables for the regression. The **R**ange **A**nalyze **R**egression command can use as many as 75 independent variables. The variables in the regression must be columns of values, meaning that any data in rows must be converted to columns with **R**ange **T**ranspose before you issue the **R**ange **A**nalyze **R**egression command.

The **Y**-Range option specifies the dependent variable. The **Y**-Range must be a single column.

The **O**utput Range option in the Regression dialog box specifies the cell in the upper left corner of the results range. This area should be an unused section of the worksheet because the output overwrites any existing cell contents.

The Y-Intercept options enable you to specify whether you want the regression to calculate a constant value. Calculating the constant is the default; in some applications, however, you may need to exclude a constant.

The results include the value of the constant and the coefficient of the single independent variable that was specified with the **X**-Range option. The results also include a number of regression statistics that describe how well the regression line fits the data.

Right Align

By default, 1-2-3 for Windows aligns labels to the left and values (numbers and formulas) to the right of the cell. You can align labels to the right side of a cell. This could, for example, improve the appearance of the column heading over a column of numbers.

To align data

1 Highlight the range and then choose **S**tyle **A**lignment. The Alignment dialog box appears.

2 In the Horizontal area of the Alignment dialog box, select the **R**ight option button.

Shortcut
Press Ctrl+R
or
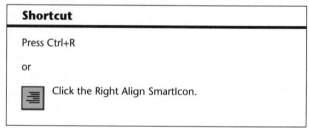 Click the Right Align SmartIcon.

3 Choose OK.

Rounding

Depending on the number format you choose, 1-2-3 for Windows may round the number that is displayed. (The original number still is used in calculations.) Changing the numeric format is one method for rounding numbers. You also can use the @ROUND function to round a number. See *Functions*.

To round values using a number format

1 Highlight the cell or range containing the value you want to round.

2 Choose **S**tyle **N**umber Format. The Number Format dialog box appears.

3 Select one of the formats from the **F**ormat list box. You can select a format by typing the initial character of the format (such as **F** for Fixed) or by using the arrow keys or the mouse.

4 If you choose Fixed, Scientific, , Comma, Currency, or Percent, you can specify the number of decimal places or use the default number, 2, shown in the **D**ecimal Places box.

To change the number of decimal places, type another number between 0 and 15 or use the scroll arrows to change the number. For some formats like General, the **D**ecimal Places text box doesn't appear in the dialog box.

5 Choose OK to close the Number Format dialog box and change the format of the selected range.

See also: *Number Formatting*

To round a value using @ROUND

1 Highlight the cell containing the value you want to round.

2 Edit the data in the contents box to read @ROUND(data,2). The word data represents the existing information in the cell, whether a value or formula. Change the 2 to any number of decimal places you want to use. If the cell contains the formula @D5*H2, for example, you would change the contents box to @ROUND(D5*H2,1) to round to one decimal place.

> **Note**
>
> If the second argument (the number of decimal places to round) is a negative number, it represents rounding to the left of the decimal point. For example, @ROUND (235.22, -1) gives the result 240.

> **Shortcut**
>
> ![0,0] Click the Comma Format SmartIcon to round a number to the nearest integer and display thousand separators (commas).

Row Heights

By adjusting row heights, you can make worksheet entries more attractive and easier to understand. The default row height, which depends on the default font, changes if you change the global font. For example, if the global font is 10-point Arial, the default row height is 14 points. If you change the global font to 14-point Arial, the default row height changes automatically to 17 points. A *point* is approximately 1/72 of an inch when printed; therefore, 12-point type is about one-sixth of an inch high when printed.

1-2-3 for Windows adjusts row height automatically to accommodate changes in point size. Occasionally, however, you may need to change a row's height—for example, you may need to add more white space between rows of data. The following sections describe this process.

To set the default row height
You can change the row height for the entire worksheet by using the **S**tyle **R**ow Height command. In the Row Height dialog box, enter the address **A1..A8192** in the **R**ow(s) text box. Type the new row height, in points, in the **S**et Height To text box. Press Enter or choose OK.

To set individual row heights
You can change the height of a single row by placing the cell pointer in that row, then using the **S**tyle **R**ow Height command and typing the desired height into the Set Height To text box in the Row Height dialog box. Press Enter or choose OK when finished.

You can change the height of several rows by selecting a range that includes the rows before you issue the command. All rows represented in the range will be affected when you use the **S**tyle **R**ow Height command.

1-2-3 shows the column width in the date/time/style indicator in the status bar. If your indicator shows the date and time, click it once to display the column width and row height.

To change the height of an individual row, use these steps for the mouse:

1 Move the mouse pointer to the row border (below the row number in the worksheet frame) until the mouse pointer changes to a double arrow pointing vertically.

2 Press and hold down the left mouse button.

3 Drag the row border up or down to its new position and release the mouse button.

When you use the mouse to change the height of a row, 1-2-3 for Windows displays a solid horizontal line that moves with the mouse pointer and shows you the position of the new row border. You can change several rows at once with the mouse by clicking on the first row's number and dragging to highlight additional rows. Next, adjust the height of any one of the highlighted rows. All highlighted rows comply with your changes.

To change row heights in Group mode

Individual row heights can apply to several worksheets if you first group them together with Group mode. When you group worksheets together, any formatting change (such as setting row heights) that you make to one worksheet in the group affects all the worksheets in that group.

Saving Files

When you create a new worksheet file or when you make changes to an existing file, your work exists only in the computer's memory. If you don't save a new worksheet or the changes you make before you exit 1-2-3 for Windows, you lose your work. Using a Save command to save a file copies the file from memory onto the disk.

To save a file

1 Choose File **S**ave or **F**ile Save **A**s.

> **Shortcut**
>
> Press Ctrl+S
>
> or
>
> Click the Save File SmartIcon.

2 If you select **F**ile **S**ave or click the Save File SmartIcon and the file has been saved previously, 1-2-3 saves the file under the current file name without displaying a dialog box.

3 If you select **F**ile Save **A**s (or if you are saving a new file for the first time and use **F**ile **S**ave or click the Save File SmartIcon), 1-2-3 for Windows displays the Save As dialog box, in which you specify the file's name, drive, directory, and file type.

After you specify the save information, choose OK or press Enter. If an existing worksheet file already uses the file name you enter in the Save As dialog box, 1-2-3 displays a message saying that the file already exists. Choose **R**eplace to overwrite the existing file; choose **B**ackup if you want 1-2-3 to make a backup copy of the file; or choose Cancel to cancel the save operation.

You also use the Save As dialog box to assign a password or save only a selected range of cells in the current worksheet.

To save a portion of a file

The **S**elected Range Only option in the Save As dialog box saves data from a cell, range, or worksheet to a new or existing worksheet file. You might use this command to save part of a file before you change it, to break a large file into smaller files, to create a partial file for someone else to work on, or to send information to another file. For example, you may want to use this feature to break a large budget file into separate files, each one containing information about a single department's budget. This technique is useful when you need to work with portions of a worksheet's data in separate worksheet files.

The **S**elected Range Only option copies all settings associated with the copied cells, including styles, formats, protection status, range names, column widths, row heights, fonts, and font characteristics.

To save a selected range, follow these steps:

1 Choose **F**ile Save **A**s. The Save As dialog box appears.

2 In the File **N**ame box, enter a name for the file in which you want to save the range.

3 Choose the **S**elected Range Only check box in the Save As dialog box.

4 Choose OK. 1-2-3 displays the Save Range As dialog box.

5 Select the F**o**rmulas and Values option button or the Val**u**es Only option button. When you save a range by using the F**o**rmulas and Values option, 1-2-3 for Windows adjusts the addresses in formulas to reflect their new locations in the destination file. The Val**u**es Only option, on the other hand, saves all calculated cells as values.

If you save a range that contains a formula, be certain to include all the cells that the formula refers to; otherwise, the formula does not calculate correctly. If the cells you are saving are part of a named range, you must select the entire range; otherwise, the range name does not refer to the correct cell addresses.

6 Click OK or press Enter to complete the saving process.

1-2-3 saves the specified range in the specified file. 1-2-3 *doesn't* automatically open the file. To view the file, use the **F**ile **O**pen command to open the file.

Remember that 1-2-3 for Windows also enables you to copy and move data between worksheet files with the **E**dit Cu**t**, **E**dit **C**opy, **E**dit **P**aste, and **E**dit Paste **S**pecial commands. In some cases, using these commands may be just as easy as saving a range of cells.

To save files in other 1-2-3 formats

Using the Save As dialog box, you can save a 1-2-3 Release 5 for Windows worksheet file in a WK1 (1-2-3 for DOS Release 2) format by choosing the 1-2-3 (wk1) option in the File **T**ype drop-down list box. You can also save a file in the WK3 (1-2-3 for Windows Release 1 or 1-2-3 for DOS Release 3) format by choosing the 1-2-3 (wk3) option. Choosing these options adds the WK1 or WK3 extension to the file name. If you prefer, you can simply type the file name with the WK1 or WK3 extension in the File **N**ame text box.

Although saving 1-2-3 for Windows files in 1-2-3 WK1 or WK3 format is possible, you lose some of the worksheet information in the conversion because 1-2-3 Release 5 supports features that earlier releases of 1-2-3 do not support.

1-2-3 Release 5 for Windows enables you to save files in several other formats, which are listed in the File **T**ype drop-down list box. The file types include SmartMaster (t4), Shared (ns4), Text (txt), Excel Workbook (xlw), Excel Worksheet (xls), dBase (dbf), and Paradox (db). To save a worksheet in one of these formats, type the file name and file extension in the File **N**ame text box of the Save As dialog box, and then click OK.

See also *Naming Files*.

To automatically save files

If you want 1-2-3 to automatically save open files at time intervals, choose **T**ools **U**ser Setup. In the User Setup dialog box, choose the **S**ave Files Every [__] Minutes check box. Specify a number of minutes in the spin box, and then choose OK. At the specified time interval, 1-2-3 will save the open files; if a file has not been named, the Save As dialog box appears at the first save interval. After you name the file, 1-2-3 continues to save the file at the specified time interval. To disable this feature, deselect the same check box.

Sending Mail

Electronic mail systems allow you to communicate with other users of electronic mail by sending and receiving files and messages through your computer. To use electronic mail, your computer must be connected to a computer network or have access to a computer network running an electronic mail program. You can send mail from 1-2-3 with Lotus Notes, cc:Mail for Windows, VIM mail applications, and Microsoft Mail.

Send

Files that you send via electronic mail are just like other files; you don't need to save them in a special way or with a unique file extension. You just need to know the complete file name and in which directory the file is located. If you do not want to send an entire file, you can send a chart, map, drawn object, or range in a mail message. You can also send a mail message from 1-2-3 without any attachments.

To send a mail message

1 Choose **F**ile Send **M**ail. The Send Mail dialog box appears.

Shortcut
Click the Send E-mail SmartIcon.

2 Select the Message Only option button.

3 Choose OK. A dialog box from your mail application appears. Continue by using the send method for your mail application.

To send an object with mail

1 Select the chart, map, drawn object, or range (to be sent as a picture).

2 Choose File Send Mail. The Send Mail dialog box appears.

3 The third option button is already selected and indicates the kind of object you have chosen, such as Drawing or Chart or Range. If you selected a range to insert as a picture, choose the Send as Picture check box.

4 Choose OK. A dialog box from your mail application appears. Continue by using the send method for your mail application.

To attach a 1-2-3 file with mail

1 Open the file you want to attach to a mail message.

2 Choose File Send Mail. The Send Mail dialog box appears.

3 Select the Save and Attach File option button.

If the file has already been saved and not further modified, the option is called Attach File.

4 Choose OK.

If the named file has been modified, 1-2-3 saves the file. If the file has not yet been named, the Save As dialog box appears. Name and save the file.

5 A dialog box from your mail application appears. Continue by using the send method for your mail application.

Range Routing

New with Release 5 of 1-2-3 for Windows is *range routing*, which enables you to send a range of a worksheet to a list of other mail users in succession. Each person in the list can make changes to the range and then send the range to the next recipient in the list, and eventually back to the originator, if that option is selected. Alternatively, the range can be routed to all recipients on the list at one time.

To send a range with mail

1 Open the worksheet and select the range you want to send with your mail message.

2 Choose **F**ile Send **M**ail. The Send Mail dialog box appears.

The Range option button is already selected, showing the range address you selected.

> **Note**
>
> If you want to use range routing, do *not* choose the Send as Picture check box. See the earlier section, "To send an object with mail," to send a range as a picture.

3 Choose OK. The Send Range As dialog box appears.

4 Select an option button to send the range as either **F**ormulas and Values, which leaves formulas intact, or **V**alues Only, which converts formulas to their values.

5 Choose OK. The Send Mail worksheet appears. Your range selection appears, surrounded by gray.

In the top left corner of the worksheet, below the SmartIcon palette, is the message box, which already contains your name (as defined in User Setup) and the current date.

6 If the edit cursor does not already appear in the message box, double-click the message box. Enter a message. The recipient will receive this message along with the worksheet range.

7 Choose the Send button. The Send dialog box appears.

8 In the To list box, enter the names of the mail recipients. You can separate the names with commas or press Enter after each name.

If the range is to be routed to a list of recipients in order, enter the names in the order they are to be sent.

If the list of names exists in the address book, choose the **A**ddress button. Highlight the names, and then choose Inse**r**t Address to add the names to the To text box.

9 In the drop-down box, select Route To Addresses In Sequence to send to the first recipient in the To list box. The range will be routed to the second person when the first person chooses Send, and so on until all recipients have received the range.

Or, to send to all recipients in the To list box at the same time, select Send To All Addresses At Once.

10 In the S**u**bject text box, enter a subject, which will appear as the title of the Send Mail worksheet and as the subject of the mail message to the recipients.

> **Tip**
>
> Choose **O**ptions to select other mail delivery and tracking options. You can choose the Return to **O**riginator check box to add your name to the end of the list of recipients. When the range has been routed to the list, you receive the range with a Merge button, or if the range was sent to all recipients at once, a Reply button is added to the worksheet.
>
> Track the location of a routed range by choosing the **R**eturn Receipt and Track check box. A delivery confirmation is sent to each person on the list when the next person receives the mail, and the originator receives a copy of the file at each step.
>
> If you chose **O**ptions, choose OK to return to the Send dialog box.

11 Choose **S**end. 1-2-3 sends the range according to the addresses and options you specified.

Receive

If you want to be notified when you receive mail while you are in 1-2-3 for Windows, you must:

- Indicate in your mail application, such as Lotus Notes or cc:Mail, that you want to be notified.

- Have your mail application currently running while you are in 1-2-3.

Received mail is announced by the appearance of the envelope icon on the mail button in the status bar. There may be a short delay from the time mail is received by your mail application until you see the indicator in 1-2-3.

To read new mail in 1-2-3

1 Click the mail button on the status bar.

2 Select a message to read.

3 Exit the mail application to return to 1-2-3.

To receive a mailed range

1 Click the mail button on the status bar.

2 Select and open the message that contains the range that was mailed to you. The mail message includes a comment from the sender and an icon for the attached 1-2-3 file containing the range.

3 Select the 1-2-3 icon and choose **F**ile Save **A**s to save the 1-2-3 file to a specified drive and directory. Open the 1-2-3 file in 1-2-3 for Windows. The Send Mail worksheet is displayed.

Message boxes are displayed, including the name and a comment from each person who is on the routing list. The range of data is also displayed.

4 Edit the data in the range.

5 Add comments to the message box that has your name at the top.

6 Choose one of the following, depending on how the file was sent:

- If you were the originator of the routed range, choose Merge to copy the range to your original worksheet, after the others on the list have made changes. See the next section, "To merge a routed range."

- If you are a member of a routing list, choose Route. The Route dialog box appears and displays the name of the next person on the route list. Choose OK to save the file and send it to the next person on the list.

- If the range was routed to all recipients simultaneously, choose Reply. The Confirm Send dialog box appears and displays the name of the originator of the file. Choose OK to save the file and mail it back to the sender.

To merge a routed range

1 Open the file that was mailed to you. The Send Mail worksheet is displayed.

2 If you do not want to merge the whole range, which will overwrite the data in the range, highlight the part of the range that you want to merge.

> **Note**
>
> You can't merge a range that is completely outside the original worksheet range, or a range that is larger than the original range. If the new range is larger, you can create a version (see *Version Manager*) or copy the data and paste it to another location in the worksheet (or another sheet).

3 Choose Merge. The Merge dialog box appears.

4 Choose OK. The Merge Options dialog box appears.

5 Choose **K**eep Both if you want to save both new and existing data as versions of the original range.

Or choose **R**eplace to replace the original data in the range with the new data.

A message box is added to the Send Mail worksheet with information about this merge.

6 Repeat steps 2 through 5 if you want to merge other ranges of the new data into the original worksheet. An additional message box is added to the Send Mail worksheet for each merge operation.

7 Choose **F**ile **C**lose or double-click the control menu box to close the Send Mail worksheet.

SmartIcons

SmartIcons are on-screen buttons you can use to make many 1-2-3 for Windows tasks easier. Instead of moving through several layers of menus to choose commands, you can click a SmartIcon to initiate the action. You need a mouse to use SmartIcons because you cannot access them from the keyboard.

SmartIcons are grouped together into *palettes* you can display on-screen. The Default Sheet palette (the one that appears on-screen after you start 1-2-3) includes SmartIcons that perform a wide range of common tasks. You aren't limited, however, to the SmartIcons displayed in the Default Sheet palette; you can choose between several standard palettes. You can also customize a palette to display the SmartIcons you use most often.

SmartIcon Basics

To use a SmartIcon, place the mouse pointer on the SmartIcon, and click the left mouse button once. This click invokes the SmartIcon's action. Depending on the SmartIcon's exact purpose, you may want to select data or otherwise prepare the worksheet before clicking the SmartIcon. If you want to apply boldface formatting to a range of data, for example, you should select the range before you click the Boldface SmartIcon.

If you are not sure what action is associated with a SmartIcon, place the mouse pointer over the SmartIcon. A bubble appears next to the SmartIcon with a description of that SmartIcon's function. To see the description of another SmartIcon, move the mouse pointer over that SmartIcon. If the bubble descriptions do not appear on your screen, turn on the feature by choosing **T**ools SmartIcons. In the SmartIcons dialog box, select the S**h**ow Icon Descriptions check box, and then choose OK.

Using SmartIcon Palettes

As you work in 1-2-3, you notice that the SmartIcon palette changes from time to time, depending on your actions. 1-2-3 switches among four default SmartIcon palettes. If you work with ranges, the Default Sheet palette appears. If you work with charts, drawn objects, or query tables, the Default Chart, Default Arrange, or Default Table palettes appear, respectively. If you select a range or a cell, the Default Sheet palette reappears.

To switch SmartIcon palettes

Along with its default palettes, 1-2-3 provides optional SmartIcon palettes. You can switch among the optional palettes in several ways. First, you can click the SmartIcons selector in the status bar at the bottom of the screen. After you click this button, a list of all the optional palettes appears (including any custom palettes you have created).

Select the desired palette from this list, and 1-2-3 immediately replaces the current palette with the one you selected. You can switch among these palettes at any time.

> **Shortcut**
>
> To cycle through the SmartIcon sets in the palette list, click the Select SmartIcons SmartIcon, which appears at the far right end of some palettes.

You also can switch among SmartIcon palettes by using the **T**ools Smart**I**cons command. Follow these steps:

1 Choose **T**ools Smart**I**cons. The SmartIcons dialog box appears, as shown in the following figure.

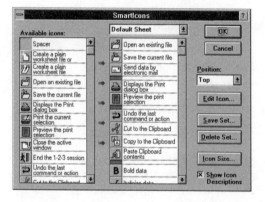

2 Click the drop-down list at the top of the dialog box. This list contains the names of the optional and custom SmartIcon palettes.

3 Select the desired palette from the list.

4 Choose OK.

To hide the palette

You may want to hide the palette if you require maximum screen space for a worksheet. To hide the palette, you can choose the Hide SmartIcons option in the palette list (the list that appears after you click the SmartIcon selector in the status bar). You also can hide the SmartIcon palette by choosing the **V**iew Set View **P**references command and then deselecting the SmartIcons check box.

After hiding the palette, you can display it again by choosing the Show SmartIcons option from the palette list. You also can choose the **V**iew Set View **P**references command and then select the SmartIcons check box.

To change the palette position

You can move the SmartIcon palette around the screen if you don't like its position. You can position the palette on any side of the screen or make it "float" within the program window. To move the palette, follow these steps:

1 Choose **T**ools SmartIcons. The SmartIcons dialog box appears.

2 Click the **P**osition drop-down list to display a list of positions (Floating, Left, Top, Right, and Bottom).

3 Select the desired position.

4 Choose OK.

If you choose the Floating option, you can click and drag the palette around the screen. You also can change the size and shape of the palette by dragging its borders.

To rearrange SmartIcons in a palette

If you don't like the arrangement of SmartIcons in a palette, you can rearrange them to suit your needs. Just hold down the Ctrl key as you click a SmartIcon in the palette, drag the SmartIcon to a new position, and then release both the mouse button and the Ctrl key.

Shortcut

 Click the Customize SmartIcons SmartIcon.

To add or remove SmartIcons

1 Choose **T**ools Smart**I**cons. The SmartIcons dialog box appears.

2 In the drop-down list at the top of the dialog box, select the SmartIcon palette that you want to modify. The SmartIcons in the selected palette appear below the name of the palette.

3 In the Available Icons list, locate the SmartIcon that you want to add.

4 Click the SmartIcon, drag it across to the palette list, and then release the mouse button. The SmartIcon appears in the palette where you dropped it.

To remove a SmartIcon from a palette, drag it out of the palette list.

You can change the order of the SmartIcons by dragging them to different positions in the palette list.

> **Tip**
>
> Use the Spacer SmartIcon (at the top of the Available Icons list) to separate SmartIcons into groups within a palette. You can use as many spacers as you choose.

To save a modified palette

If you save your changes to a palette, the new version of the palette is available the next time you use 1-2-3 for Windows. To save the changes you made to a set of SmartIcons, follow these steps:

1 Click the **S**ave Set button in the SmartIcons dialog box. 1-2-3 for Windows displays the Save Set of SmartIcons dialog box.

2 To change the name of the SmartIcon set, type a new name in the **N**ame of Set text box.

3 To change the file name, type a new file name in the File Name text box.

4 Click OK to close the Save Set of SmartIcons dialog box. You return to the SmartIcons dialog box.

5 Click OK to close the SmartIcons dialog box and return to the worksheet.

To delete a palette

You can delete SmartIcon palettes by selecting the **D**elete Set button in the SmartIcons dialog box. The Delete Sets dialog box appears. In the list box, select each palette you want to delete. Choose OK to delete the selected palettes.

To change the size of SmartIcons

You can display SmartIcons in two sizes: medium and large. By default, 1-2-3 for Windows displays medium-sized SmartIcons. To change the size of SmartIcons, follow these steps:

1 Choose **T**ools Smart**I**cons. The SmartIcons dialog box appears.

2 Click the **I**con Size button to access the Icon Size dialog box.

3 Select the **M**edium or **L**arge option button.

4 Choose OK to close the Icon Size dialog box. You return to the SmartIcons dialog box.

5 Choose OK to close the SmartIcons dialog box and return to the worksheet.

Editing SmartIcons

The new icon editing feature enables you to create a new icon, paint an icon to change its colors, assign a macro to a custom icon, or modify an existing icon. If you want to use an icon that is a bitmap from outside 1-2-3, copy it to the Clipboard before choosing Tools SmartIcons. You cannot modify the standard 1-2-3 SmartIcons; however, you can use a standard SmartIcon as a starting point for creating a new icon.

To create a new icon

1 Select a cell, range, chart, drawn object, or query table. The icons available in the SmartIcons dialog box vary based on the current selection. For example, you will not see the charting SmartIcons unless you select a chart.

2 Choose **T**ools SmartIcons. The SmartIcons dialog box appears.

> **Shortcut**
>
> Click the Customize SmartIcons SmartIcon.

3 Choose the **E**dit Icon button. The Edit Icon dialog box appears.

4 Choose the **N**ew Icon button, or, if you are using an icon from the Clipboard, choose the Paste **I**con button. The Save As a New Icon dialog box appears.

5 Type a file name in the text box. Choose OK. A blank icon is presented in the Edit Icon dialog box.

6 Type a description for the icon in the **D**escription text box.

See the next sections for painting the icon and assigning a macro to it.

> **Tip**
>
> You can create new icons by using existing 1-2-3 icon images as a starting point. Just select the image in the Available Icons list box (on the left side of the Edit Icon dialog box), choose Save **A**s to assign a name for the icon, and then use the edit area to change the original.

7 Choose OK. The icon appears in the Available Icons list box and can be added to a palette.

To paint an icon

1 In the Edit Icon dialog box, select an icon or create a new icon as described earlier.

2 Click the arrow beside the color palette to view more colors for the icon. Click any color to select it. The currently selected color(s) appear on the mouse icon.

Click the right mouse button on a color if you also want to use the right mouse button for painting.

3 Use the mouse to draw in the edit area using the color you selected. You can click a bit at a time to color individual pixels.

You can erase parts of your image by selecting the background color and drawing over existing colors. Look at the Preview box to see how the icon will look in actual palette size.

4 Choose OK. The new or modified icon appears in the Available Icons list box.

To assign a macro to an icon

1 Choose **T**ools Smart**I**cons. The SmartIcons dialog box appears.

2 Choose the **E**dit Icon button. The Edit Icon dialog box appears.

3 In the Available Icons list box, select the icon to which you want to assign or change a macro.

4 Enter the macro in the **E**nter Macro Here text box.

> **Tip**
>
> If the macro exists in a worksheet or elsewhere, you can copy it to the Clipboard, then choose Paste **M**acro to place the macro in the **E**nter Macro Here text box.

5 Choose OK to close the Edit Icon dialog box. Choose OK to close the SmartIcons dialog box.

To modify an existing custom icon

1 Choose **T**ools Smart**I**cons. The SmartIcons dialog box appears.

2 Choose the **E**dit Icon button. The Edit Icon dialog box appears.

3 Select the icon you want to modify in the Available Icons list box. The icon appears in the enlarged view box.

4 Paint the icon to change its appearance. See the earlier section, "To paint an icon."

5 Modify the macro attached to the icon. See the earlier section, "To assign a macro to an icon."

6 Choose OK to close the Edit Icon dialog box. Choose OK to close the SmartIcons dialog box.

SmartMasters

When you start 1-2-3 for Windows, one of the options in the Welcome to 1-2-3 dialog box is **C**reate a New Worksheet. The New File dialog box appears when you select this option, and each time you choose **F**ile **N**ew. You can choose whether to start with a blank worksheet or with a SmartMaster worksheet template.

The SmartMasters are a collection of impressive templates for some popular spreadsheet uses, such as expense reports, personal budgets, mortgage amortization, time sheets, and more. Each SmartMaster contains sample data to demonstrate how the SmartMaster works. Click the Information sheet tab for more help with the SmartMaster.

SmartMasters give you a head start on developing an effective worksheet. You can modify existing SmartMasters and

214 SmartMasters

save them as new templates, or create new custom Smart-Masters using the Shell SmartMaster.

To create a new file using SmartMasters

1 Choose **F**ile **N**ew. The New File dialog box appears.

> **Note**
>
> If the New File dialog box does not appear, the option has been turned off in user setup. You can use either of these methods to create a new file using a SmartMaster:
>
> - Choose **T**ools **U**ser Setup. In the User Setup dialog box, deselect the **S**kip New File And Welcome Screens check box. Choose OK, and then try **F**ile **N**ew again.
>
> - Choose **F**ile **O**pen to open a SmartMaster template. Change to the \123R5W\MASTERS directory and select SmartMaster (wt4) in the File **T**ype list box. Select the File **N**ame you want, noting the Comments box that describes it. Choose OK to open the SmartMaster. Be sure to save as a worksheet instead of as a SmartMaster. Skip the remaining steps 2 and 3.

2 Highlight a SmartMaster from the Create A Worksheet By Selecting A **S**martMaster list box.

A description of the highlighted item appears in the Comments box. The file name for the selected Smart-Master appears at the bottom of the dialog box.

> **Note**
>
> The default directory for the original 1-2-3 SmartMasters is \123R5W\MASTERS. If you want to open a template that was saved to a different directory, choose the **B**rowse button to select the file in the Browse dialog box. When you choose OK, the file name is displayed in the New File dialog box.

3 Choose OK. 1-2-3 creates a new file based on the selected SmartMaster, using a default file name.

The following figure shows one of the sheets of a worksheet file based on the Generate Financial Statements SmartMaster.

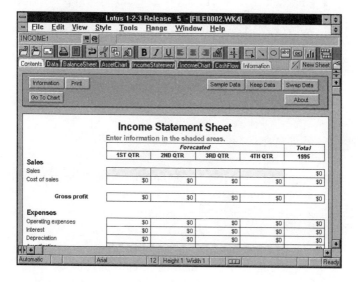

To save a file based on a SmartMaster

1 Choose File Save As. The Save As dialog box appears.

2 Change directories if you want to save a file to a different directory than the one shown. In the File Name text box, type a name to replace the default file name.

3 In the **C**omments text box, the comment describing the SmartMaster appears. Edit as needed.

4 Choose OK.

To create a customized SmartMaster

1 Choose **F**ile **N**ew. The New File dialog box appears.

> **Note**
>
> If the New File dialog box does not appear, the option has been turned off in user setup. Choose **F**ile **O**pen to open a SmartMaster template. Change to the \123R5W\MASTERS directory and select SmartMaster (wt4) in the File **T**ype list box. Select the File **N**ame you want, noting the Comments box that describes it. Skip step 2.

2 Highlight a SmartMaster from the Create A Worksheet By Selecting A **S**martMaster list box.

> **Tip**
>
> If none of the SmartMasters resembles the SmartMaster you want to create, choose the SmartMaster called Use Shell To Create a SmartMaster, which is an "empty" template that still contains the helpful buttons and professional design of the other SmartMasters. Follow the directions on the Contents sheet to begin. The Information Index on the Information sheet tab is also helpful in setting up the SmartMaster.

3 Choose OK. The SmartMaster template is opened.

4 Modify the SmartMaster to customize it for your use as a new SmartMaster template.

5 Choose OK. 1-2-3 creates a new file based on the selected SmartMaster, using a default file name.

6 Choose **F**ile Save **A**s. The Save As dialog box appears.

7 Change directories if you want to save a file to a different directory than the one shown.

It is suggested that you save the SmartMaster to the \123R5W\MASTERS directory to make the SmartMaster readily available when you create new files.

8 In the File **T**ype drop-down list, choose SmartMaster (wt4) to save the file as a SmartMaster.

9 In the File **N**ame text box, type a name to replace the default file name. 1-2-3 will supply the necessary WT4 extension.

10 In the **C**omments text box, type a comment to describe the new template.

11 Choose OK. The file is saved as a SmartMaster template.

12 Choose **F**ile **D**oc Info. The Doc Info dialog box appears.

13 In the **T**itle text box, type a title for the new SmartMaster. This title and the comments will appear in the **S**martMaster list box in the New File dialog box.

14 Choose OK.

Solver

The Solver analyzes data and data relationships in a worksheet to determine a series of possible answers to a specific problem. At your request, the Solver determines the optimal answer of all answers found, and shows you how each answer was derived.

To use Solver

1 Choose **R**ange Analyze **S**olver. The Solver Definition dialog box appears.

> **Shortcut**
>
> Click the Solver SmartIcon.

2 The **A**djustable Cells and **C**onstraint Cells text boxes initially display the cell pointer's current location in the worksheet.

3 To complete the problem description, specify a set of **C**onstraint Cells.

4 Click the **S**olve button to start the search for solutions.

The Solver Progress dialog box displays when a solution search is in progress. In this box, the Stop button enables you to stop a search for solutions at any time. Solver retains all solutions found before you click the Stop button.

From the Solver Answer dialog box, the **D**efinition option button returns you to the Solver Definition dialog box. The Answ**e**r option button displays information about the answers found. The **R**eports option button enables you to choose a report type.

By successively clicking the **N**ext button, you can cycle through all the solutions the Solver found. Each time you display a new solution, the data in the worksheet changes to reflect the new solution. Clicking the **O**riginal button at any point returns the initial worksheet values from which the search for solutions was launched. Click the **F**irst button to return to the first answer.

After Solver finds one or more solutions, exit from Solver by repeatedly clicking the Close button in the Solver Answer dialog box. Before you click the Close button, however, decide which solution you want to leave on the worksheet. Select a solution with the **N**ext button, and then click the Close button. You can save the displayed solution for future reference. If you prefer to save the solution separately, create a sheet in the current worksheet file and place the selected solution in the new worksheet file.

When the Solver looks for answers to a problem, it presents only those answers for which all constraints are true. When Solver can't find an answer for which all constraints are true, it presents what it calls an *attempt*—that is, the best solution given that one or more constraints cannot be satisfied. Solver presents attempts in the Solver Answer dialog box the same way it presents answers. Click the **N**ext button until you find the attempt that seems most reasonable, given what you know about the problem.

If there is a chance that Solver can find an answer, a **G**uess button appears in the Solver Answer dialog box, enabling you to supply more information to Solver about the adjustable cells in the problem. Click the **G**uess button to display the Solver Guess dialog box. You can accept the suggested value for the current adjustable cell, or enter a new value. Continue this process for all adjustable cells by clicking the Next Cell option. Then click the **S**olve button. Solver tries to find an answer to the problem based on the new information you provide.

Although the Solver Answer dialog box can cycle through Solver's answers quickly and display supporting data in the worksheet, you might find it more useful to display the Solver's results in a report. After the Solver finds answers to a problem, click the **R**eports option button in the Solver Answer dialog box, which displays the Solver Reports dialog box. If you choose options in this dialog box, you can generate seven different kinds of reports on the answers found by Solver.

For detailed examples using Solver, refer to Que's *Using 1-2-3 Release 5 for Windows*, Special Edition.

Sorting Ranges

You can use the **R**ange **S**ort command to sort ranges of data in 1-2-3 for Windows. To sort data, you must specify the keys for the sort. The field with the highest precedence is the first key, the field with the next-highest precedence is the second key, and so on. You can use up to 255 keys in a sort.

220 Sorting Ranges

To sort a range using a single key

1 Select the range you want to sort.

   If you are sorting records in a database table, do not include the field names. Do include all columns, to avoid scrambling the data.

2 Choose **R**ange **S**ort. The Sort dialog box appears.

3 In the **S**ort By text box, enter the address of one cell in the column by which you want to sort.

   You can also use the cell selector to click a cell in the column.

4 Choose either **A**scending or **D**escending sort order.

> **Shortcut**
>
>   Click the Ascending Sort or Descending Sort SmartIcon.

5 Press Enter or click OK.

If sorting on a single key does not sort the data in the order you need, use multiple sort keys to specify additional sorting conditions.

To sort a range using multiple keys

1 Select the range you want to sort.

2 Choose **R**ange **S**ort. The Sort dialog box appears.

3 In the **S**ort By text box, enter the address of one cell in the column by which you want to sort.

   You can also use the cell selector to click a cell in the column.

4 Choose either **A**scending or **D**escending sort order.

Shortcut

   Click the Ascending Sort or Descending Sort SmartIcon.

5 Click the Add **K**ey button, and repeat steps 3 and 4 to specify additional sort keys.

6 Choose OK.

Specifying Ranges

Many commands act on ranges. When 1-2-3 for Windows prompts you for a range, you can respond in one of three ways:

- Type the addresses of the corners of the range or of the cells in the ranges.

- Highlight the range with the keyboard or the mouse, before or after you select the command.

- Type the range name or press Name (F3) and select the range name, if one has been assigned. Or click the Navigator and select a range name from the drop-down list.

The following sections describe these options in detail.

To type a range address

The first method of specifying ranges, typing the address, is used the least because it is most prone to error. With this method, you type the addresses of any two cells in diagonally opposite corners of the range, separating the two addresses with one or two periods.

To highlight a range

Highlighting a range in Point mode is the most popular method of identifying the range. You can highlight a range with the keyboard or the mouse, either before or after you issue a command.

When you preselect cells and then issue a command, the address automatically appears in the dialog box. You don't have to enter the address again. One exception exists; when you group worksheets together with Group mode, the default range is the three-dimensional range that spans the whole group, even if you have preselected a range in only one worksheet. To override the default range in this case, you must type the range address.

If you are using the keyboard to preselect a range, press F4 and highlight the range, using the arrow keys. When you finish specifying the range, press Enter. Using the Shift key can make the selection process even faster. Just move to the beginning of the range, press and hold the Shift key, then press the arrow keys as necessary to highlight the rest of the range. When you finish, release the Shift key. This method also works if you are selecting the range after issuing the command.

To highlight a range with the mouse, just click any corner of the range, then drag to the diagonally opposite corner. All cells between the corners will be highlighted. You can also click on a corner, hold the Shift key down, and then click on the opposite corner.

To highlight a collection

You can highlight a group of ranges, called a *collection*. Just highlight the first range using any method you like, then hold the Ctrl key down as you highlight other ranges. All ranges will become highlighted as a *collection*.

To specify a range after issuing a command

If you forget to select a range beforehand, you can select one after you issue the command. When the command leads to a dialog box, you can type or point to the range within the dialog box. The method of pointing is faster and easier than typing range addresses. Also, because you can see the cells as you select them, you make fewer errors by pointing than by typing.

To highlight a range after issuing a command, highlight the existing range entry inside the dialog box, and then click and drag on the worksheet to highlight the desired range. The reference of the range you highlight will replace the old reference.

Alternatively, you can click the *range selector* to specify a range within a dialog box that contains a range text box. This action removes the dialog box temporarily while you select the desired range in the worksheet. The dialog box reappears when you finish selecting the range or press Enter.

If you have named the range, you can type the range name where a range address is required. You can also use the Navigator to supply a range name when you want to enter a range in a formula. See also *Naming Ranges*.

Spell Checking

1-2-3 includes a handy spelling-checker utility that reviews and helps you correct spelling throughout your worksheet files.

To activate the spelling checker

1 Choose **T**ools **S**pell Check. The Spell Check dialog box appears.

> **Shortcut**
>
> Click the Check Spelling SmartIcon.

2 Select the area of the worksheet that you want to spell check—the **E**ntire file, the **C**urrent worksheet, or a specific r**a**nge.

3 Choose the **O**ptions button to specify your preferences. A list of options for your application appears.

4 Click OK to return to the Spell Check dialog box.

224 Spell Checking

5 When you're ready, choose OK to begin checking the selection. If the spelling checker finds an unknown word, a dialog box appears. Using the options in this box, you can correct the mistake or otherwise deal with the item.

You can enter a replacement word in the Replace **W**ith text box and then choose **R**eplace to continue, or you can use one of the **Al**ternatives provided by 1-2-3. Double-click the desired alternative in the list to use it.

The spelling checker may flag some correctly spelled words as incorrect, simply because those words are not in the spelling checker's dictionary. You can add those words to the dictionary by clicking the **A**dd To Dictionary button. By adding words to the dictionary, you begin to create your own personal dictionary for repeated use.

Spell check indicates with a message box that the spell check is complete. Choose OK.

Splitting the Worksheet Window

See *Worksheet Views*

Starting 1-2-3 for Windows

You can start 1-2-3 for Windows by selecting its *application icon*. The 1-2-3 for Windows icon may be in a separate group window, called Lotus Applications, or it may be located in the Windows Applications group window. If you chose to install the 1-2-3 for Windows Translate program, the Dialog Box Editor, Macro Translator, Guided Tour, or the Country Sorting Tool, these application icons are located in the same group window.

If the 1-2-3 for Windows icon is contained in a group window that is itself an icon, you must use the File **R**un command to start 1-2-3 or open the group-window icon by double-clicking on it so that you can select the 1-2-3 for Windows application icon.

To start 1-2-3 for Windows
To start 1-2-3 for Windows with a mouse, move the mouse pointer to 1-2-3's application icon and double-click the left mouse button.

To start 1-2-3 with the keyboard, first make certain that the window containing 1-2-3's application icon is the active window. If that window is not active, press Ctrl+Tab until it is (or select the group window name from the Program Manager's **W**indow menu). Then use the direction keys to highlight the icon. Finally, press Enter to run 1-2-3.

You also can start 1-2-3 for Windows by choosing the **F**ile **R**un command from Program Manager. The Run dialog box appears. Type **C:\123R5W\PROGRAMS\123W.EXE** in the **C**ommand Line text box, and press Enter. (If you chose to install 1-2-3 for Windows in a different directory, substitute that directory name instead.)

1-2-3 displays a copyright banner as it starts, and then a blank worksheet appears, upon which the Welcome to 1-2-3 dialog box opens. The **C**reate a New Worksheet option opens the New File dialog box, where you can choose a Smart-Master template for the new worksheet. The **W**ork On An Existing Worksheet option opens the Open File dialog box, where you can select an existing file. Choose the QuickStart Tutorial button to start a tutorial. Choose Cancel to remain in the Untitled worksheet.

If you want to skip the Welcome to 1-2-3 dialog box on starting 1-2-3, choose **T**ools **U**ser Setup. In the User Setup dialog box, choose the **S**kip New File And Welcome Screens check box, and then choose OK. With this option selected, 1-2-3 skips both the Welcome dialog box and the New File dialog box; an Untitled worksheet is opened.

Style Gallery

Like the named-style feature, the **S**tyle **G**allery command allows you to apply styles quickly to a selected range of cells. The difference between the named-style feature and the Style Gallery is that the Style Gallery contains 14 predesigned style templates. Just choose a template from the list in the Gallery dialog box and all the style characteristics that make up the template are applied to the selected range.

Shortcut

 Click the Style Gallery SmartIcon.

To remove a template from the selected range, choose **E**dit Cl**e**ar **S**tyles Only.

Shortcut

 Click the Delete Styles SmartIcon.

Refer to the Sample area in the Gallery dialog box to preview each template before applying it to the selected range.

Styling Data

To change the style characteristics of a cell or cell range, first select the cell or range and then choose any of the first four commands on the **S**tyle menu: **N**umber Format, **F**ont & Attributes, **L**ines & Color, or **A**lignment. Choose style options from the dialog box that appears.

When you apply style characteristics to a cell, indicators for some of the style characteristics appear on the status bar. The status bar lets you quickly change certain style characteristics for the selected cell or range without choosing menu and dialog box options. Click the attribute you want to change in the status bar, and 1-2-3 displays a pop-up list of selections. Use the mouse or the arrow keys to choose an item from the pop-up list.

If you have applied styles to a cell or range and would like to easily reuse the same attributes, you can name the style. See *Named Styles*. You can also copy the styles of a cell by choosing the **S**tyle Fas**t** Format command. First, highlight the cell whose styles you want to copy to another range. Choose **S**tyle Fas**t** Format. The mouse pointer becomes a paint brush. Click the cells or drag the ranges to which you want the styles applied. To turn off the formatting, choose **S**tyle Fas**t** Format again or press Esc.

> **Shortcut**
>
> Click the Fast Format SmartIcon.

See also *Number Formatting*, *Fonts and Attributes*, *Lines and Colors*, and *Aligning Data*.

Subtotals

The @SUBTOTAL function is used to mark values for the @GRANDTOTAL function. The @SUBTOTAL function adds a list of values and returns the sum, similar to the @SUM function (see next section on *Summing*). The syntax for the @SUBTOTAL function is as follows: @SUBTOTAL(*list*).

The @SUBTOTAL function is a tool that allows you to mark and gather specific groups of data. A common use of this function lists range names in the argument, separated by commas, to mark larger totals for the @GRANDTOTAL function. Only the @SUBTOTAL formulas are used in @GRANDTOTAL. Any @SUM formulas in the range are ignored by @GRANDTOTAL.

Summing

The most common worksheet function is the @SUM function. 1-2-3 for Windows provides the Sum SmartIcon to quickly sum a column or row of numbers.

To sum numbers automatically

1 Select a cell next to the range you want to sum.

2 Click the Sum SmartIcon.

1-2-3 for Windows creates a sum formula and selects the range it thinks you want to sum. The @SUM function appears in the contents box. The result appears in the cell.

> **Tip**
>
> You can also select a range in which you want to enter sum formulas and click the Sum SmartIcon to create several sum formulas at once.

To use the @SUM function

1 Highlight the cell into which you want to place the formula.

2 Type **@SUM(**.

3 Highlight the range to sum. 1-2-3 for Windows puts the range in the formula.

4 Press Enter. The result appears.

See also *Functions*.

Templates

See *SmartMasters*

Text Blocks

Text blocks are useful for many worksheet tasks. You can use a text block to hold headings or titles for your worksheet reports. You can use text blocks to hold annotation information, or even create simple layouts with text blocks. If you want to add an explanation to your worksheet, create a text block. A text block can point out key information. The following sections explain how to manipulate the text inside a text block.

To create a text block

1 Choose **T**ools **D**raw **T**ext.

> **Shortcut**
>
> Click the Text Block SmartIcon.

You are prompted to click and drag to draw a text block. A text block is the container for your descriptive text.

2 To draw the text block, place the mouse pointer on the chart or worksheet in which you want the text to go, and then click and drag to create a box the approximate height and width of the text block you are entering.

3 After drawing the box, type the text in the block. To enter multiple lines of text, either let the text word wrap or press Enter after each line.

> **Tip**
>
> To move the text block, click the block to select it. Then touch the mouse pointer to the border and drag the block to the new location.

To edit text in a text block

1 Double-click the text block. A cursor appears at the beginning of the text.

2 Use the mouse or arrow keys to position the cursor and make corrections.

3 Click outside the text block.

230 Text Blocks

> **Note**
>
> If you don't make your text block long enough, your text may scroll out of view after you type another line. If this happens, you must lengthen the block by dragging the center handle at the bottom of the selected text block.

To change the font and attributes of a text block

1 Click the text block to select it.

2 Choose **S**tyle **F**ont & Attributes. The Font and Attributes dialog box appears.

> **Shortcut**
>
> Click the Font & Attributes SmartIcon.

3 Select the effects you want. See *Fonts and Attributes* for more information.

Note that you cannot format individual characters inside the block; it's all or nothing.

4 Choose OK when you are finished.

To change the interior color of a text block

1 Click the text block to select it.

2 Choose **S**tyle **L**ines & Color. The Lines and Color dialog box appears.

> **Shortcut**
>
> Click the Lines & Color SmartIcon.

3 Select the effects you want. See *Lines and Colors* for more information.

4 Choose OK when you are finished.

To align text inside a text block
1 Click the text block to select it.

2 Choose **S**tyle **A**lignment. The Alignment dialog box appears.

3 Choose an option. You can use only horizontal alignment within a text block; you cannot align text vertically in a text block.

4 Choose OK.

To delete a text block
1 Click the text block to select it.

2 Press Delete.

See also *Drawing*.

Totals

See *Summing*

Underlining

You can select from three styles of underlining in 1-2-3 for Windows. Or choose even more line styles if you use the border feature to add a line to the bottom or top of cells, rather than underlining the text in the cells. Another alternative is to use the line drawing tool to draw a line freehand, and then choose options to change the color and width of the line.

To underline text
1 Highlight the cells containing text to be underlined.

2 Choose **S**tyle **F**ont & Attributes. The Font & Attributes dialog box appears.

232 Underlining

> **Shortcut**
>
> Click the Font & Attributes SmartIcon.

3 In the Attributes area, check the **U**nderline check box. In the drop-down box, choose from single underline, double underline, or a thick single underline. The Sample box shows how the underline and other attributes you select will look in the worksheet.

> **Shortcut**
>
>   Click the Single Underline or Double Underline SmartIcon.

4 Choose OK.

See also *Fonts and Attributes*.

To use borders for underlining

1 Highlight the cells to which you want to add a bottom border. If you prefer, you can highlight cells below the row you want to underline, and add a top border.

2 Choose **S**tyle **L**ines & Color. The Lines & Color dialog box appears.

> **Shortcut**
>
> Click the Lines & Color SmartIcon.

3 In the Border area, check the Botto**m** check box. In the Line st**y**le drop-down box, select a line style. In the Line color drop-down box, select a color for the line. The Sample box shows how the border will look in the worksheet.

4 Choose OK.

See also *Borders*.

To draw lines for underlining

1 Choose **T**ools **D**raw **L**ine.

> **Shortcut**
>
> Click the Draw Line SmartIcon.

After you select the line drawing tool, the mouse pointer changes to a cross and 1-2-3 prompts you to click and drag to draw the line or arrow.

2 Place the cross at the location where you want the line to begin. Hold down the Shift key (to keep the line straight) and then click and drag to where you want the line to end.

3 After you reach the end of the line, release the mouse button. The line has handles at each end, indicating it is selected.

4 Touch the mouse arrow to the line and then click the right mouse button to display the quick menu.

5 Choose Lines & Color from the quick menu. An abbreviated version of the Lines and Color dialog box appears.

6 Make selections from the St**y**le, **W**idth, and **C**olor drop-down boxes.

7 Choose OK.

> **Tip**
>
> You can change the length of the drawn line by dragging a handle (while holding down the Shift key). You can reposition the line by clicking the line (not on a handle) and dragging it.

See also *Drawing*.

Undo

If you change the worksheet in error, you can choose **E**dit **U**ndo to reverse the change. The Undo feature undoes only the last action performed.

> **Shortcut**
>
> Press Alt+Backspace or Ctrl+Z
>
> or
>
> Click the Undo SmartIcon.

To use Undo properly, you must understand what 1-2-3 for Windows considers to be a change. A change occurs between the time 1-2-3 for Windows is in Ready mode and the next time 1-2-3 for Windows is in Ready mode.

This feature requires a great deal of computer memory; how much memory depends on the different actions involved. If you run low on memory, you can disable the Undo feature by using the **T**ools **U**ser Setup command and deselecting the **U**ndo option.

Version Manager

The Version Manager provides easy-to-use "what-if" analytical power that lets you create and view different sets of data for any named range. Each different set of data you create is called a *version*. To make it easier to manage versions, you also can group versions of different ranges together to create *scenarios*.

Version Manager provides two tools for working with versions and scenarios: the Manager and the Index. Each of these tools appears in the Version Manager window. The Manager lets you create, display, modify, and delete versions. The Index lets you do everything the Manager does *plus* create and manage scenarios, create reports, and merge versions and scenarios from one file into another.

Using the Manager

Choose **R**ange **V**ersion. The Version Manager window appears.

Shortcut
Click the Version Manager SmartIcon.

To create a version

1 Enter the data for the version. If the range already contains data you want to preserve, begin by creating a version that contains the data currently stored in the range.

This action saves the data so that you don't lose the original data when you enter different sets of data for the range. You can create versions only of named ranges. You can choose **R**ange **N**ame to assign a name to a range; see *Naming Ranges*. Or you can use the **C**reate button in the Manager window.

2 Open the Version Manager and select the **C**reate button. The Create Version dialog box appears.

For the **R**ange Name, Version Manager suggests a name based on the label in the worksheet or suggests a default name such as RANGE1. For the **V**ersion Name, Version Manager suggests a default version name, such as Version1.

3 Type a **R**ange Name and a **V**ersion Name in the text boxes (or keep the suggested names).

4 In the **C**omment text box, type a comment that helps you remember why you entered the data in this version.

5 In the Sharing Options area, you can choose the **P**rotected option button to protect versions so that other users can't change them. Choose the Protected & **H**idden option button if you want to hide versions so that other users can't display them. If you are not sharing the data, you may keep the default option, **U**nprotected.

6 Choose OK to create the version and return to the Version Manager window.

The name of the range appears in the Named **R**ange drop-down list box. The name of the version appears in the With **V**ersion(s) drop-down list box in the Manager window.

7 To create a second version of a range, begin by entering the data for the new version into the worksheet. As soon as you enter new data in the range, the check mark next to the version name in the Manager window changes to a crossed check mark, the version name appears in italic, and the Update button becomes available.

8 Repeat steps 2 through 6 to record the new version.

To display versions

1 Choose **R**ange **V**ersion. The Version Manager window appears.

2 In the Named **R**ange drop-down list box, select the desired range. In the With **V**ersion(s) drop-down list box, select the desired version.

1-2-3 for Windows places the data for that version of the range into the worksheet, replacing any data already there.

> **Caution**
>
> When a crossed check mark appears next to a version name, the current data in the range has not been saved in a version. Displaying a different version in that range destroys the current data in the range. Choose the **C**reate button to create a new version that includes the current data, or choose the **U**pdate button to update the current version with the data in the range.

3 Select other versions as desired for comparison of the data.

To modify and update versions

1 Display the version in the worksheet (see "To display versions," above).

2 Enter the new data for the version.

3 Choose the **U**pdate button in the Version Manager window. The Update Version dialog box appears.

4 Choose OK.

To change a version's comment, sharing options, and style-retention setting, display the version in the worksheet and then choose the **I**nfo button from the Version Manager window. The Version Info dialog box appears. Edit the Comment text box and change other settings for the version.

Using the Index

Choose **R**ange **V**ersion. The Version Manager window appears. Select the **T**o Index button (located on the right side of the Manager window) to open the Version Manager Index window. The object list in the center of the window contains information about the versions and scenarios in the current file. The buttons above the object list let you change the way the list is displayed or the information it contains.

To use the Sort selector

The first time you open the Index window, the text on the Sort selector button is Range Name S**o**rt, indicating that the list is sorted by range name. You can sort the object list by version name, scenario name, date, and user name in addition to the default range-name sort. Click the Sort selector button and choose a sort order from the drop-down list.

> **Tip**
>
> Make more of the Index window visible by maximizing. Click the Maximize button in the top right corner of the Index window.

To use the Shown selector
The Shown selector button, which contains the text All Show**n** the first time you open the Index window, lets you control which versions (and scenarios, in a scenario-name sort) 1-2-3 includes (or "shows") in the list. Click the Shown selector button and choose from the drop-down list which versions you want shown.

To select and display versions in the Index window
In the Index window, you can select several versions at once on which to perform actions. To select multiple versions, click on the first version and then hold down the Ctrl key while clicking additional versions. To select a group of adjacent versions, click on the first version and drag the mouse pointer over the other versions you want to select.

With a version or multiple versions selected, you can choose any of the following buttons at the bottom of the Index window

- The **S**cenario button to group the versions together into a scenario

- The **I**nfo button to change sharing options and style-retention settings for the versions

- The **D**elete button to delete the versions

- The Sho**w** button to display the versions

To display a single version in the worksheet when you are using the Index window, double-click on it in the object list. To display multiple versions, select the versions and then choose the Sho**w** button.

To create, display, and modify scenarios
  1 Choose the **S**cenario button in the Index window. The Create Scenario dialog box appears.

  2 In the **A**vailable versions list box, select a version, then click the << button. The versions you select appear in the Selected **v**ersions list box.

> **Shortcut**
>
> You can also double-click each version in the **A**vailable versions list box to move the version to the Selected versions list box.

3 Choose OK. The Index window automatically changes to the scenario-name sort.

4 From the list of scenarios in the Index window, double-click the scenario you want to display, or select it and choose Sho**w**.

5 To edit a scenario's comment, change its sharing options, or change the versions included in the scenario, select the scenario name from the Index window list, and choose **I**nfo. The Scenario Info dialog box appears.

6 Edit the text boxes and other options as needed, and then choose OK.

> **Tip**
>
> You can modify sharing options for several scenarios at once if you select all the scenarios from the Index window list, and then choose Info to display and modify the scenarios.

For more information on using the Version Manager, refer to the Lotus 1-2-3 Release 5 for Windows documentation or the 1-2-3 Release 5 for Windows Help system.

What-If Tables

What-if tables enable you to work with variables whose values are not known. Worksheet models for financial projections often fall into this category. With the **R**ange **A**nalyze **W**hat-if Table command, you can create tables that show how the results of formula calculations vary as the variables used in the formulas change.

In 1-2-3 for Windows, a *what-if table* is an on-screen view of information in column format, with the field names at the top. A what-if table contains the results of a **R**ange **A**nalyze What-if Table command plus some or all the information used to generate the results. A *what-if table range* is a worksheet range that contains a what-if table.

A *variable* is a formula component whose value can change.

An *input cell* is a worksheet cell used by 1-2-3 for Windows for temporary storage during calculation of a what-if table. One input cell is required for each variable in the what-if table formula. The cell addresses of the formula variables are the same as the input cells.

An *input value* is a specific value that 1-2-3 for Windows uses for a variable during the what-if table calculations.

The *results area* is the portion of a what-if table in which the calculation results are placed. One result is generated for each combination of input values.

The formulas used in what-if tables can contain values, strings, cell addresses, and functions. You should not use logical formulas because this type of formula always evaluates to either 0 or 1. Although the use of a logical formula in a what-if table does not cause an error, the results generally are meaningless.

With the **R**ange **A**nalyze **W**hat-if Table command, 1-2-3 for Windows can generate three types of what-if tables. The three table types differ in the number of formulas and variables they can contain. Descriptions of the table types follow:

1 variable	One or more formulas with one variable; generates a 1-dimensional table.
2 variables	One formula with two variables; generates a 2-dimensional table.
3 variables	One formula with three variables; generates a 3-dimensional table.

To create a 1-variable what-if table

1 Select a location for the table range.

2 Select a location outside the table range for the input cell and label it.

3 Use the first row of the table range to enter one or more formulas, making sure that each formula refers to the input cell.

4 Beginning in the second cell in the first column of the table range, enter the input values 1-2-3 will use in the formulas. Make sure that you leave the top left cell of the table blank.

5 Choose **R**ange **A**nalyze **W**hat-if Table.

6 Choose 1 from the **N**umber of Variables drop-down list.

7 Specify the table range in the **T**able Range text box (this is the range that contains all formulas and all input values).

8 Specify the input cell in the Input Cell **1** text box.

9 Choose OK.

To create a 2-variable what-if table

1 Select a location for the table range.

2 Select a location outside the table range for the input cells and label each location.

3 Use the top left cell of the table range to enter the formula. Make sure that the formula refers to both input cells.

4 Begin with the cell under the formula in the first column of the table range and enter the input values associated with input cell 1.

5 Enter the input values associated with input cell 2 in the cells to the right of the formula.

6 Choose **R**ange **A**nalyze **W**hat-if Table.

7 Choose 2 from the **N**umber of Variables drop-down list.

8 Specify the table range in the **T**able Range text box.

9 Specify the input cells in the Input Cell **1** and Input Cell **2** text boxes.

10 Choose OK.

To create a 3-variable what-if table

1 Insert as many worksheets as you need to equal the number of values for input cell 3.

2 Select a location for the table range.

3 Select a location outside of the table range for the input cells and label each location.

4 Use a cell outside of the table range to enter the formula to be analyzed. Make sure that the formula refers to all three input cells.

5 Using the first worksheet, in the first column of the table range, enter the values related to input cell 1. Make sure that you copy these values to all worksheets in the table range.

6 In the first worksheet and the first row of the table range, enter the values related to input cell 2. Make sure that you copy these values to all worksheets in the table range.

7 In the top left corner cell of the table range, enter one input value for input cell 3 in each worksheet.

8 Choose **R**ange **A**nalyze **W**hat-if Table.

9 Choose 3 from the **N**umber of Variables drop-down list.

10 Specify the table range in the **T**able Range text box.

11 Specify the input cells in the Input Cell **1**, Input Cell **2**, and Input Cell **3** text boxes.

12 Specify the formula cell location in the **F**ormula Cell text box.

13 Choose OK.

Worksheet Views

You can change the way that 1-2-3 for Windows displays multiple worksheet windows so that you can, for example, compare data in two or more worksheet files or open utility windows within a worksheet or chart.

You also can change the way you view an individual file within a worksheet window. These options, described in the following sections, enable you to compare data within a worksheet and to see different parts of your work at the same time.

To split the worksheet window

You can split a window either horizontally or vertically into two *panes*. This technique is useful if the worksheet is larger than the screen can display and you want to see different parts of the worksheet at the same time. The technique is also useful if you need to display several windows at the same time but want to see a larger area of one window.

To split a window, follow these steps:

1 Select a cell where you want to split the screen horizontally or vertically. The position of the cell pointer determines the size of each window.

Do not position the cell pointer at the first or last row or column that is visible in the worksheet window.

2 Choose **V**iew Split. The Split dialog box appears.

3 Choose **H**orizontal for a horizontal split, or **V**ertical for a vertical split.

To split a window with the mouse, point to the horizontal splitter (just above the vertical scroll bar) and click and drag the pointer down to divide the window into two horizontal panes, or click and drag the vertical splitter (just to the left of the horizontal scroll bar) to create two vertical panes.

In a split window, you can change data in one pane and see how the change affects data in the other pane. This capability is quite useful for what-if analysis.

At times, you may want to see two unrelated views of the same worksheet. In this case, you want the two panes to scroll separately. Use the **V**iew **S**plit command and deselect **S**ynchronize Scrolling in the Split dialog box to make scrolling *unsynchronized*; select the **S**ynchronize Scrolling option if you want to restore synchronized scrolling. To move between panes, use the Pane (F6) key or click in the other window with the mouse.

Because a split window displays two frames, you cannot display quite as much data at one time as you can with a full window. You can remove the frames by choosing **V**iew Set View **P**references and deselecting the **W**orksheet Frame option in the View Preferences dialog box, but the two panes may be more difficult to separate visually, and the address of the current cell will be less obvious.

To clear a split window

To clear a split window, choose **V**iew C**l**ear Split. No matter which pane the cell pointer is in when you choose this command, the cell pointer moves to the left or upper pane when you clear a split window.

To display worksheets in perspective view

You can display up to three worksheets in a file simultaneously in 1-2-3 for Windows; this type of display is called *perspective view*. To show a file in perspective view, follow these steps:

1 Choose **V**iew **S**plit. The Split dialog box appears.

2 Choose the **P**erspective option.

> **Shortcut**
>
> Click the Perspective View SmartIcon.

You can have a split window or a perspective view, but not both at the same time.

To freeze titles

Most worksheets are much larger than can be displayed on-screen at any one time. As you move the cell pointer, you scroll the display. New data appears at one edge of the display while the data at the other edge scrolls out of sight. Data can be hard to understand when titles at the top of the worksheet and descriptions at the left scroll off the screen.

To lock titles on-screen, follow these steps:

1 Position the worksheet so that the titles you want to lock are at the top and to the left of the display.

2 Move the cell pointer to the cell in the first row below the titles and in the first column to the right of the titles.

3 Choose **V**iew Freeze **T**itles. The Freeze Titles dialog box appears.

4 You can lock the top rows with **R**ows, the leftmost columns with **C**olumns, or both rows and columns with **B**oth.

To unlock the titles, choose **V**iew Clear **T**itles. To change the locked area, choose **V**iew Clear **T**itles and then specify the new titles area.

If you press Home when titles are locked, the cell pointer moves to the position below and to the right of the titles rather than to cell A1. When you move the mouse pointer into the titles area, you cannot select any cells. You cannot use the direction keys to move into the titles area either, but you can use GoTo (F5).

In a split window, locking titles affects only the current pane. Unless you are using Group mode, locking titles affects only the current worksheet in a file.

Zooming the Display

By using the **V**iew Set View **P**references command and changing the Custom **Z**oom % setting in the Set View Preferences dialog box, you can specify a percentage (anywhere from 400 to 25) by which to enlarge or shrink the worksheet display. Select 400 to make the worksheet four times larger; select 25 to make the display shrink to one-fourth its normal size. If you reduce the display, the resulting image is barely readable, but it gives you a long-range view of many cells. The readability of these settings varies from monitor to monitor.

You can use three commands in the **V**iew menu—**Z**oom In, Zoom **O**ut, and **C**ustom—to switch among different zoom percentages.

Shortcut
Click the Zoom In and Zoom Out SmartIcons.

Index

A-B

addresses, 9, 49-50, 221
aggregates, 66-67
alignment, 13-15, 22-23, 116, 192, 231
Approach, 16
arguments, 102, 130-131
ASCII text files, 182

backgrounds, 36, 134
Backsolver, 18-19
bin range, 101
boldfacing, 20
borders, 20-22, 117, 232

C

cells
    addresses, 9
    boldfacing, 20
    borders, 20-22
    centering data, 22-23
    Clip Art, importing, 38-39
    copying to a range, 51
    current, 7
    entering data, 85-88
    erasing, 88-89
    formulas, 98-100
    hiding, 186-187
    numbers, 69-71, 164-168
    prefix (centering entries), 23
    protecting, 185
    saving, 197-198
    styles, 226-227
    text wrap, 15
    underlining, 231-233
charts, 24-38
    axes scale, 35
    columns, 26
    data labels, 36-37
    defaults, 27
    displaying (F5), 28
    frames, resizing, 30
    graphics, 106
    legends, 32-33
    maps, 131-137
    modifying, 31-37
    naming, 28
    notes, 33-34
    objects, 29-31
    orientation, 32
    printing, 37-38
    ranges, 25-27
    resizing, 28-31
    rows, 26
    selection handles, 27
    titles, 33-34
    types, 31-32
circular references, 190-191
Clip Art, 38-39, 106
Clipboard, 39-40, 48
codes (maps), 132
collections (ranges), 222
colors, 117-118
    grid lines, 107
    icons, 212
    maps, 134
    text blocks, 230
columns, 7
    charts, 26
    data, 14-15, 22-23
    deleting, 72-73
    hiding, 187-188
    inserting, 114
    recalculation, 189-190
    width, 41-44
commands
    macros, 130-131
    selecting, 139-142
compressing text, 177-178
contents box (edit line), 9
context-sensitive help, 111-112
control bar, 9
copying, 46-52, 81-83
criteria formulas, 63
crosstabs, 16, 65-67
current cell, 7
cursor, 85-88
custom dialog boxes, 73-77
customizing
    fill sequences, 93-94
    legends, 32-33
    SmartIcon palettes, 208
    SmartMasters templates, 216-217
cutting ranges, 80, 89, 144-145

D

data entry, *see* entering data
Database functions, 105
databases
    crosstabs, 65-67
    defining, 56-58
    external connections, 67-77
    fields, 56-59
    labels, 57
    Notes, 163-164
    records, 56-65
dates (ranges), 91-92

debugging macros, 126-127
decimal places (numbers), 69-71
deleting
    borders, 22
    cells, 88-89
    chart objects, 30-31
    columns, 72-73
    drag-and-drop, 89
    decimal places, 70
    fields, 59
    files, 71
    headers/footers, 110
    named styles, 147
    numbers, 70
    objects, 83
    palettes, 210
    passwords, 184-195
    ranges, 88-89
    records, 59, 64-65
    rows, 72-73
    SmartIcons, 209
    text boxes, 231
    worksheets, 72-73, 153
dialog boxes, 73, 141-142
Dialog Editor, 73-77
directories, 24
display mode (windows), 5
displaying
    background grids, 36
    charts (F5), 28
    file information, 54
    scenarios, 238-239
    SmartIcon palettes, 208
drag-and-drop
    copying, 47-48
    deleting, 89
    moving, 143-144
    objects, 82-83
drag-and-fill ranges, 94
drives, 169
drop shadows (borders), 22

E

edit line, 9-12
editing, 157
    data, 84
    macro buttons, 130
    shortcut (F2), 59
    SmartIcons, 210-234
    text blocks, 229-230
electronic mail, 199-205
ellipses, 79
embedding, 118-122, 163-164
entering
    data, 85-88
    functions, 102
    labels, 85-87
    values, 87-88
ERR message, 104
expanding text, 177-178
extensions (files), 148-149
external connections (databases), 67-77

F

@function selector, 104
fields (databases), 56-59
file-navigation keys, 158
files
    ASCII text, 182
    closing, 40-41
    combining values, 44-45
    copying, 48
    creating, 53-54
    custom fill sequences, 93
    databases, 58
    deleting, 71
    directories, 24
    electronic mail, 200
    extensions, 148-149
    memory, 40-41
    naming, 147-149
    opening, 169-172
    protecting, 182-188
    saving, 196-199
    SmartMaster, 53, 215-217
    worksheets, 6-7, 53-54
fill sequences, 92-94
finding and replacing, 94-96
fonts
    attributes, 96-97
    maps, 136
    points, 96-97
    row heights, 194-195
    text boxes, 230
    typefaces, 96-97
footers, 109-110, 178-179
formatting
    copying, 52
    numbers, 69-71, 164-168, 192
formulas, 98-100
    auditing, 16-18
    Backsolver, 18-19
    circular references, 190
    copying, 50-51
    criteria formulas, 63
    functions, 102-106
    labels, 85-87
    variables, 240
frames, 30, 180
freezing titles, 100-101, 245-246
frequency distributions, 101
function selector, 9
functions, 102-106, 192-194, 227-228

G-H

graphics, 38-39, 106
grid lines, 36, 107-108, 180
Group mode, 44, 108, 195

headers, 109-110, 178-179
    centering, 22-23
    margins, 137
    text blocks, 228-231
help, 111-112
highlighting, 64, 221-222

I-J

icons, 211-214
importing
    Clip Art, 38-39
    data, 112-113
input cells, 240
inserting
    columns, 114
    fields, 59
    notes (charts), 33-34
    page breaks, 175-176
    records (databases), 59
    rows, 114
    worksheets, 114
installing 1-2-3, 115-116
inverting matrices, 138
iterations (recalculations), 190

K-L

key fields (databases), 56-57

labels
    alignment, 13-15
    axes, 35
    charts, 36-37
    databases, 57
    formulas, 85-87
    mailing, 16
    numbers, 85-87
    prefixes, 86-87
    range names, 151
landscape orientation, 177
legends, 32-33
lines, 78-79
linking, 118-121

M

macros, 122-131
maps, 131-137
margins, 137, 181
matrices, 137-138
memory, 40-41
menu bar, 9
menus, 138-142
merging, 204-205
mixed addresses, 50-51
mode indicator (status bar), 10
modifying
    icons, 213-214
    records, 65
    scenarios, 238-239
multiplying matrices, 138

N

named styles, 146-147
natural order recalculation, 189-190
navigation, 153-163

Navigator, 9, 153-154
Notes, 163-164
notes in charts, 33-34
numbers
    decimal places, 69-71
    formatting, 164-168
    formulas, 98-100
    labels, 85-87
    rounding, 70, 192-194
    scientific notation, 88
    values, 87-88

O-P

objects, 29-31, 80-83, 200
OLE (Object Linking and Embedding), 118-121
opening files, 169-172, 183
operators, 63, 98-100
orientation, 15, 32, 177

page breaks, 175-176
page setup, 174-175
palettes (SmartIcons), 205-213
passwords, 183-195
pasting ranges, 144-145
prefixes, 23, 86-87
printing, 173-182
    charts, 37-38
    grid lines, 108
    previewing, 37-38
Program Manager, 115

Q-R

query tables, 59-60, 65-67
quick menus, 138-142

range selector, 223
ranges
    addresses, 221
    anchoring, 175
    bin range, 101
    borders, 20-22
    copying to cells, 51
    creating charts, 25-27
    custom fill sequences, 93
    cutting, 144-145
    data labels, 36-37
    drag-and-fill, 94
    electronic mail, 201-203
    erasing, 88-89
    filling, 90-94
    hiding, 186-187
    highlighting, 221-222
    maps, 135
    moving, 142
    naming, 149-151
    navigating, 153-154
    numbers, 69-71, 164-168
    pasting, 144-145
    printing, 175-178
    protecting, 185
    routing, 201-205

saving, 197-198
sorting, 219-221
specifying, 221-223
summing, 105
transposing, 52
Version Manager, 234-239
recording macros, 124-125
records (databases)
deleting, 59, 64-65
fields, 56-57
highlighting, 64
inserting, 59
modifying, 65
searching, 62-65
sorting, 60-62
viewing, 16
rectangles, 79
regression analysis, 190-191
relative addressing, 49
reserving files, 185-186
rows, 7
charts, 26
date/time/style indicator, 42
deleting, 72-73
heights, 194-195
hiding, 187-188
inserting, 114
recalculation, 189-190, 190
running macros, 125-126

S

saving, 181, 196-199, 215-216
scenarios (Version Manager), 234-239
scientific notation, 88
scrolling, 244
searching, 62-65
Shell (SmartMasters), 216-217
Show selector (Version Manager), 238
Single Step mode, 127
SmartIcons, 10, 205-213
SmartMaster, 53, 213-217
Solver, 217-219
Sort Selector, 237
sorting
data, 16
ranges, 219-221
records, 60-62
spell checking, 223-224
starting 1-2-3, 224-225
Statistical functions, 106
status bar, 10-11
styles, 51-52, 145-147
subdirectories, 169
Subtotal function, 227
Sum function, 227-228
summing ranges, 105
switching windows, 6

T

tables, 239-243
tabs, 154
Task LIst, 6

templates, 213-217
text, 15, 177-178
creating, 78
editing, 229-233
Text functions, 106
tiling windows, 5
title bar, 9
titles
charts, 33-34
freezing, 100-101
maps, 135
printing, 180
text blocks, 228-231
worksheets, 245-246

U-V

underlining, 231-233

values
alignment, 13-15
combining, 44-45
entering, 87-88
variables (formulas), 240
Version Manager, 234-239
viewing
records, 16
worksheets, 243-246

W

what-if tables, 239-243
width (columns), 41-44
wild cards, 62-63, 170
windows, 3-6, 10
worksheets
deleting, 72-73
embedding (Notes), 163-164
files, 6-7
grouping, 108-109
hiding, 187-188
inserting, 114
naming, 151-153
navigating, 153-163
recalculating, 188-190
splitting, 243-244
tabs, 154
titles, 245-246
viewing, 243-246
wrapping text, 15

X-Y-Z

X-Axis dialog box, 35-83

Y-Axis dialog box, 35-83
zooming, 246